SDd

ROBIN MAGOWAN

Improbable
Journeys

THE MARLBORO PRESS | NORTHWESTERN
NORTHWESTERN UNIVERSITY PRESS
Evanston, Illinois

The Marlboro Press/Northwestern
Northwestern University Press
Evanston, Illinois 60208-4210

Printed in the United States of America

10 9 8 7 6 5 4 3 2 1

ISBN 0-8101-6092-7

Library of Congress Cataloging-in-Publication Data

Magowan, Robin.
    Improbable journeys / Robin Magowan.
        p. cm. — (Marlboro travel)
    ISBN 0-8101-6092-7 (alk. paper)
    1. Magowan, Robin—Journeys. 2. Voyages and travels. I. Title.
    II. Series.
    G465 .M333 2002
    910.4—dc21

                                                    2002001016

The paper used in this publication meets the minimum requirements of
the American National Standard for Information Sciences—Permanence of
Paper for Printed Library Materials, ANSI Z39.48-1984.

FOR JULIET YLI-MATTILA

Contents

Introduction

All writers risk their identities, some with each sentence. But when one is writing about a life of another culture that can't help but seem elusive, the charlatan in oneself may feel all too exposed. Limited to the surface, to the most fortuitous of impressions, how can a pair of foreign eyes hope to pen anything that can vie with what an insider, born there, carrying its landscape in his bones, might write?

One answer, I suppose, is to make the most of necessity. The local writer is, after all, clothed: clothed in his historical understanding, his particular class, his various loyalties. But the outsider is naked, and therein lies an advantage. By deliberately stripping myself of my culture and making myself vulnerable, I am allowing myself to be touched and, to a certain degree, transformed. How open, the traveler asks, can I be? What else, I say, looking wildly about, can I embrace?

We judge a travel writer by what he takes in, the quality and inclusiveness of his embrace. And we judge him by the courage with which in his ignorance he proceeds, his ability to make himself into a vessel that a foreign life can imprint. If there is an art to travel writing, perhaps it consists in conjuring ever more ingenious ways of stripping the self so it can be cracked open. This alone lets the writer understand new people and places, not to mention the old self, the old world of home. In all travel writing there is a two-way tug, a constant reference to a life, a readership, left behind.

The two-way tug is one of the heart. In any love affair with a foreign culture, there is inevitably an undercurrent of transgression that borders on the erotic. I am intruding where I have no business, across minefields and gates that have to be coaxed, if not forced, open. To see anything at all I must find a way of breaking out of the no-man's-land of hotels and restaurants and museums in which they have me quarantined, where the locals would never dream of venturing.

Once out of the tourist zone, new obstacles arise. Who are you but a much-awaited fatted calf? No one need think twice about relieving you of your wherewithal. The local economy may well depend on how much your go-betweens can extract; their problem is how to do it without being contaminated. For uncontacted peoples, the stranger is someone suspect, to be sacrificed and eaten on the spot. But there are laws of hospitality: might you be that fabled rarity, a god in disguise? To reassure, you may mutter something about the places that have received you, or haul out your *cartes d'identité*, the much-scribbled-over four-by-six pack. While traveling, there are worse things to be accused of than ambition: aim high enough and—who knows?— you may actually arrive.

As in a love affair, or a religious quest, I want to do more than merely arrive. My whole being is predicated on getting as far inside as I possibly can, for knowledge depends on my navigating forbidden waters. The French travel poet Victor Segalen sums up the yearning to span the globe in an embrace—*where haven't I traveled yet? what secrets still await me?*—in a single cry:

> *Seigneur innommable du monde, donne-moi l'Autre! Le Div . . .*
> *non, le Divers. Car le Divin n'est qu'un jeu d'homme.*

Just as a man seeks out the quality of otherness in a woman— what else is her femaleness, her hair, her perfume, her body?— so the traveler searches for the quality of otherness in a country.

The Other becomes, in this sense, a guarantor of authenticity. In the act of touching it, that person, that place, that godhead, I hope to be enlarged, if not transformed.

The search for the Other contains an element of flight, of *escape toward.* I am trying to escape the trammels of class, of gender, of narrow definitions, as well as the whole climate of fear that the Other normally arouses. Where else but in the glistening mirror of another place can I learn how to see the culture that has tried to define my boundaries? Travel becomes a way of amplifying and even reinventing the self from one encounter, one journey, to the next.

Stendhal called the search for the Other that drove him *la chasse au bonheur.* Thomas Jefferson enshrined this phrase, lifted from Condorcet, in the Declaration of Independence as one of every American's three inalienable rights. Forgetting where the pursuit of happiness has brought us as a nation—isn't suffering what most people have accepted as their earthly lot? from where else can compassion spring?—I insisted, when coming of age, on nailing the quest for happiness to my voyager's mast as I tried to escape the narrowness and fear of the McCarthy-ridden 1950s.

I hoped to free myself by discovering how other people, collectively, went about trying to make themselves happy. Was it the mere attempt, the pursuit itself, they lived for? Or did some of them—at a bullfight in Spain, over a two-hour lunch in France—actually attain happiness? Does paradise exist only in the next world? Or is it, in special places and under special circumstances, to be encountered here below? Must one journey far and endure much to find it? Or, as Maeterlinck suggested, is it waiting to be discovered in one's own backyard?

Happiness, alas, is subjective, and it usually takes more than a casual knock to get mystic gates to open. Most societies protect themselves. In trying to penetrate the innermost sanctum of a cultural holy of holies, to learn what a people in their heart of hearts really are about, it helps to be conversant in language and gestures, to understand what is not being revealed. The serious traveler will have to remain in situ for more than the six weeks of most of my journeys to learn what the whole round of a year brings.

In my case I have had little choice other than to barge in and try to make something of the riot of scents and colors, the bewildering kaleidoscope of activity. In this initial confusion no observations seem to make the least sense, and what happens seems equally incidental. Faced with the squalor, the heat, the mosquitoes, no one to talk to, all that, I may feel that the whole impulse has been an expensive mistake. Better to cut my losses and board the first flight home, where I belong.

But little by little, if I can persist and stick it out, I usually find that apparent chaos has begun to assume a pattern. I may still be journeying in the dark, but there is now a coherence to events and they all point somewhere. The longer I follow them, the more the hunch grows that I am tapping into something that is bringing me, willy-nilly, into the hidden ecstasies of a people.

Not every writer likes losing himself and being tossed about on the whims of an ecstatic current. Most prefer to stand back a little and filter the variety of moments on offer. But some benefit from being both more focused and more abandoned. Let yourself go! Seize each song, each little bit of mental jazz that comes your way! An aleatory approach works if you make sure that the current that has seized you is a transparent one the reader can follow from one glimpse, one shudder, to the next. As I blunder along, it helps to have cast my net wide enough to capture the entire spectrum of a place: the vermin picked out of the food; various gnats, birds, fleas, and butterflies; and, of course, the great popular addictions—stadiums, cathedrals, market-places—wherever masses of people are drawn, however mysteriously, to celebrate in common. When I can do this, the entire journey starts to radiate with something like joy: the joy of being, in a great spectacle, seated where I am. I have moved from being a witness to being something like a participant.

In recording this metamorphosis, poetry with its intensity and compression can be of service. The finer the mesh the writing weaves, the more subtle the sensations it can register. A multilayered, rhythm-driven prose should allow dialogue between experience and the resulting verbal response. The writer need not be a masked, anonymous traveler, but rather can be someone visible, engaged to his very core.

Faced with an experience more demanding, much bigger than the self, poetry and prose become acts of fidelity: ways of responding, ways of perceiving and registering that impossible thing, the Other. Through the contact with the Other, an exchange has been made. By harnessing the technical powers of poetry and prose to make my evocations as accurate as possible, I express my gratitude to a culture.

Yet prose and poetry do pull a writer in opposite directions. In verse, compression, though vivid and evocative, often seems to lead into a blind alley. Aren't we all clearest when we expand? Isn't expansion what prose wants: to embrace as much of the spectrum of experience as possible while sustaining and even raising poetic intensity? The relaxed continuous space of prose can provide a factual underpinning, the *wheres* and *whens* that may allow poetry to soar up and up, from one heady set of commas to the next, without displacing the reader. Happiness, if at all convincing, should let its smile seem to take in everything, everything that at the moment counts. Prose gives a medium with which to register that possibility.

A songlike medium, one that lives and dies within a single, however sustained moment, brings a time scale that allows me to see a journey—and by implication my own life—as the tissue of moments that it is. In bringing me into the present, it opens things up—questions I don't normally ask, subjects such as the Other I don't allow myself to talk about—while enlarging and, I hope, transforming my sensibility.

This hope, of harnessing the powers of both lyric poetry and prose, sends me back again and again to the revision table. To avoid being obscure I must use every resource available to bring alive the transforming ecstasy that a people and a place have given me.

———

I have been describing a view developed over forty years. Let's go back to the beginning, to the experiences that made me the traveler I have become. Among my earliest memories, at the age of five, shortly after Pearl Harbor, is one of my father telling me he was about to enlist as an intelligence officer in the navy. I grew up surrounded by foreign names, mysterious elsewheres. I learned to read while following battle maps in the *New York Times,* exerting what magic I could to bring my father home safely from his carrier in the Pacific. My mother would find me prone on our library rug, crayoning the map outlines in volume 26 of the *Britannica,* in much the way a child now stares riveted at a computer monitor.

For more leisurely contemplation, there was my uncle's illustrated world stamp book: colonial soldiers, outlandish storks, palm trees, thatched huts, lagoons, and rice fields waiting to be filled in with brightly colored stamps in various denominations. And I pinned the quarterly maps of the *National Geographic* to my bedroom walls. What yearning was there, waiting to be ignited!

The first spark came in 1949, when my parents took me to Rapallo for the summer. At first it was a wrench, but I became thoroughly smitten by the sharpness of the light, the rich creamy blue of the Mediterranean sky, by an intimacy of contour and scale, a peopled ancientness till then unsuspected. Until now, America had contained everything I desired, the baseball teams I aspired to, the birds I longed to know, but here was another world, another way of talking, gesticulating, being. By comparison to the America I knew, improvising itself anew with each arrival, the postwar Europe I traveled in seemed remarkably complete, exuding an authenticity I felt in the placement of a stone, the intensity of a shadow. Instead of a haphazard hodgepodge, here were presences I trusted and from which I could learn.

I went to school abroad for most of the next two years, and when I came home, a literary wanderlust took over. Just as I had been fascinated as a child by the plant importer Douglas Fairchild's *The World Was My Garden,* so I devoured all the travel books I could find. They were my lamps, lighting up cultural mazes otherwise impenetrable. And they answered my curiosity with an almost magical insistence that place creates the people who live in it. As Goethe put it in summarizing the lure of the South, "No one wanders untouched under palm trees." And just as each *place* brought a *culture* into being, so could a traveler, in opening to its powers, transform himself. It was that Other I wanted to incorporate.

Much as travel literature fascinated me, I would never have presumed as a twenty-year-old to pick up a pen and venture forth but for Henri Michaux's *A Barbarian in Asia.* On the flyleaf I found Michaux's call to arms, added specifically for Sylvia Beach's postwar translation: "The most urgently needed science is one that will show us how to make civilizations." That whetted my curiosity—how could I turn myself into a one-man maker of civilizations? By pitting yourself, the Barbarian answers, against what you see and taking it on. "If you don't generalize," Michaux remarks, "how can you have any experience?"

There was the license I needed, and when I graduated from college in 1958 and took my initial trip as a writer to Cuba, Haiti, and Jamaica, I took along Michaux's first book of prose, *Ecuador,* intending to translate it. *Ecuador* taught me how to respond, by standing up and challenging whatever purported to be the Other. Under its impact, an apprentice work of my own emerged, a diary about learning to see: black people, tropical life, my own words as they sprang onto a page.

A year later, at the end of a European honeymoon, I stumbled upon the Alhambra. The water gardens with their spouting fountains and perforated arches kindled a response in me nothing else had. Here was paradise, a dance of life of a kind I had glimpsed only in Matisse. And it made me want to see more. With two weeks still available, my wife and I crossed the straits to Tangier, to be thrilled anew by the gardens of the king's summer palace, by the mustard gold of hats, slippers, hassocks. If this vision of paradise originated, as my wife said, in Persia, it was there we resolved to go at the first opportunity.

Three years later, while in Paris, I sent Michaux my recently published Caribbean journal, *Voyage Noir,* thinking it might amuse him to see what *Ecuador* had spawned. My homage must have struck a chord, for he called at my Ile Saint Louis hotel, only to find me out. But I made sure to be there the next day when this small, broad-shouldered former seaman with pale blue eyes and a bald seagull-like head showed up again. For the next couple of hours as we strolled along the quais, we talked of the wanderlust we shared: of India, which Michaux regarded as the most profound of civilizations and to which he would have returned but for uncertain health; of the Sudan, where he had been so happy he had written nothing—nothing, Michaux said, catching himself, but the supposedly imaginary *Au Pays de la Magie;* of Iran, where I was headed. Though he had never traveled there, he fathomed the attraction. "A people so enamored of beauty as to be virtually helpless before anything possessing it—a horse or a twelve-year-old boy."

After absorbing how Michaux thought and responded as a traveler, what intrigued me now was Iran and the possibility that country of poetry offered of a wider vocation. Shortly before leaving, I came upon Robert Byron's out-of-print *The Road to Oxiana,* an exhilarating, often hilarious account of a trip to Iran and Persian-speaking Afghanistan to seek the origins of Islamic architecture. Byron's élan took me over to the extent that all I desired was to reenact his journey. I didn't realize that much of what delighted me, the brisk tour of the forbidden mosque of Mashhad disguised as a woman, the trip to an equally off-limits tribal Firuzabad, was wholesale invention. Instead, Byron made it seem that I had merely to present my calling cards for the fabled world of the miniatures to open: lutes, roses, the odd nightingale, each welcoming gesture more expansive than the last.

Alas, the twenty-five years that had elapsed between Byron's jaunt and mine had drastically changed Persian life. After seeing their oil patrimony squandered on an array of American toys, the people to whom we owe our word *paradise* had grown understandably resentful. They could not prevent tourists from visiting the historic mosques, but they could make sure the holiest stayed undefiled. Wherever we tried to walk, we found zealots hissing at my unveiled wife or tagging along in an adhesive crowd at our heels.

Our way out was to take *paradise* literally—"any walled garden" in old Persian—and visit gardens. They, of course, proved almost as illusory as everything else in that now-you-see-it, now-you-don't high desert kingdom; but that, too, could be a plus for a young imagination.

Iran might have affected me more deeply had I not encountered Greece on the way there and back. Much as I reveled in the sensation-crammed, hold-your-breath-and-dive pools I encountered, Iran remained unavoidably opaque, not to say Asian. Whereas Greece, for all its Oriental character, seemed, in James

Merrill's telling line, composed of nothing but "Essentials: salt, wine, olive, the light, the scream."

That Easter I had walked in the Cyclades, marveling at the rocks, the fig trees, the flower-spattered fields; the surviving column that marked out a pantheistic power while creating a foil for the perspectives, the patterns of light and shadow, it brought into play: the dark blue of the water, the white blobs of distant farms and chapels, so like a northern hillside's remnant snow. From where had the labor to build them come? Was there a set of masons ceaselessly maintaining molds of curved perfect white?

So, on the island of Astipálaia, I imagined a pair of towns coming into being: one white and pointed high like the prow of a ship over hillside rubble; the other, a port of pinks, ochers, browns. The child in me playing with building blocks melted before all those curves of dome and overarching street, small and with their whites refreshingly cool, if one had feet bare enough to poke along the basil-scented passageways above a sparkling sea. A little civilization stuck, if not in the sky, then in the next best site, the lip of an old volcano. For whole mornings now I walked, absorbed by the vaulted architecture, the vertigo of white lines dripping onto harsh incandescent blue.

Before long I was head over heels in love, so much so I couldn't bear to drive back through a once adored Italy. Part of me wanted to junk everything and stay to learn Greek, the musical modes, perhaps even how to farm. But instead I went to Seattle, where I wrote "Persian Mirages."

It took me two years to get back to Greece. And then it was not Attica or Páros, but the more Asiatic Greece of Lesbos, the northernmost of the Dodecanese Islands. What drew me was an interest in ecstasy. The term, as we normally use it, holds a pejorative connotation. An ecstatic is one who "stands outside"; not outside himself, but his culture. As such, he is to be feared and belittled. A better understanding of the possibilities of ecstatic transformation is conveyed by its Arab or Hebrew equivalents: *wajd,* meaning "to find oneself," and more to my taste, *hitorerut ha nefesh,* the Hebrew "awakening of the soul." I wanted to see that spontaneous combustion of a dancer, all alone on a taverna floor, dancing a *zembeikiko.*

The *zembeikiko* is not, and probably never was, very common. A creation of the eastern Aegean, it comes from the Zebeik people, for whom it represented "the struggle with the eagle." Unlike most Islamic ecstatic dances, which employ a very quick rhythm to achieve an altered state, the *zembeikiko* consists of a heavy, pounding, intensely hypnotic nine-four rhythm. This slowness gives it the meditative quality of a dance that is part dream and part exorcism or prayer. In all of the Mediterranean there is nothing quite like it.

Much of a summer passed on Lesbos before I encountered a shepherd, George, who was willing to talk about the *zembeikiko* and take me where I might see it danced. I had no need, nor any knowledge how, to attempt to dance it myself. But you can't invade an ecstatic milieu and expect to remain invisible. Gradually, despite my demurrals, I was dragged in, further and further and, I should add, more and more drunkenly. I believed it was only when soused in several liters of retsina that I could dance with any conviction. Though I learned more, and saw more, I felt basically like a puppet on a string until, near the end of the summer, George took me to a *panegyri* at Magdalena. There, finally, in front of an elegant, portly old man to whom I hadn't so much as spoken, everything broke open and I experienced something like an initiation. That ease—or is it rightness?—has never left me. Even today, given a song I haven't danced before, I can slap and circle my way down, to my knees, to the floor, and find something essential.

———

Trying to get that ecstatic journey, and the summer that came with it, down on paper was to consume most of the next six years, spent largely in Berkeley. For most travelers a journey, once concluded, is something put behind. For the writer, the journey goes on, but now I am trying to resuscitate what has otherwise vanished, to prove, perhaps only to myself, that I have lived something momentous. More than identity rides on the outcome. It was, after all, the gleam of something written that got me traveling. If I can't bring it to life, what does that say?

Yet the better traveler I become, the harder becomes the task of writing. Either I surpass myself in some way or I pick up my field notes and try again. Each journey, presumably, has been unique; if so, it must yield a perspective of its own.

Looking back now, I can see how my perspective has evolved. *Voyage Noir,* written in the Caribbean under the spell of Michaux, was basically an apprentice work about learning how to travel. The young man, blank faced as he is, comes across as a tabula rasa, asking only to be scribbled over. Fortunately there were events such as the Castro revolution, and Haitian voodoo, prepared to do just that, and I emerged with a little chapbook.

Iran, by contrast, was an exercise in persona, Robert Byron's principally, but also those of a stream of imperial British colonialists stretching back to Gertrude Bell and *Haji Baba,* whose tone I had, willy-nilly, assumed. How well any of it wears I shudder to think, but my real subject—the country of poetry— gave me the occasion to reveal a world of desire all my own.

"Persian Mirages" was the work of a few months; that "Dancing Outside" took so much longer had to do with my attempt to bring off a work of abstract expressionist prose in which visual externals were replaced by the driving rhythm that had taken me over. I wanted to show what it felt like to hurtle through the wall of the self. To what extent I succeeded in creating a prose equivalent of those big gestural paintings in which courage is everything, I don't know. Language is a much more tradition-bound medium than paint, and I could bend it only so far.

With "Dancing Outside," I reached an impasse. Short of madness or inadvertent suicide, there was nowhere I could take it. To go on, I had to draw back and adopt a less Dionysian mode. But in becoming a more conscious being, I was able to drop the invisible *one* that had masked me and enlist the *I* that was myself. I wanted the traveler to be seen: warts, hobblings, all of it.

"Zambia" and "Madagascar" were my first attempts in this new autobiographical manner. In the first, the subject matter is mainly bars and the prostitutes who, in that barely pre-AIDS era, hung out in them. But the scene gave me a pretext to create a prose version of Matisse in a sub-Saharan Africa that colorist never got to. In "Madagascar," the design was to sketch, with the help of the lemurs I identified with, an alternative melting pot and, by extension, an alternative America. But the Red Island is a very big one and, without any wheels of my own, I didn't get far enough to grasp its totality.

In Nepal, the autobiographical element finally came across. I had become what I was walking—or rather, limping—through. It helped that, up to then, I had never walked anywhere, much less on a trek that had to cross an 18,800-foot-high pass. Everything was new to me—the Buddhist landscape, the mountains with all their unexpected pain—and its newness proved to be something I could catch, virtually step-by-step, and be changed by.

While recuperating from the Himalayas in France, I fell under the spell of a Burgundian May. The autobiographical satisfaction I had discovered in writing about the trek brought a new urge to write a longer account of my life. What, after all, did I know better? Getting started was easy, but getting it right was something else, and it took more than twenty years, spent largely abroad, before I finished *Memoirs of a Minotaur*. The issue, as it turned out, wasn't so much knowing as caring. The Other had brought a reality, something objective I cared about and felt compelled to convey. But the self, that being in constant transformation, never stayed still long enough to be known, let alone loved. No matter how much I peeled away, there was always another veil, another misunderstood layer, awaiting me.

Shortly after returning to northwest Connecticut in 1991 and buying an old farmhouse, I discovered a small outcropping a few feet from my studio. I was now of an age where I could welcome any excuse to get away from my desk to kneel in sunlight and feel part of a shifting moment. Founding civilizations may have been beyond me, but I discovered that I could be a founder of alpine plant environments.

Soon I had enough cleared that I could plant a bevy of miniature plants culled from every possible high mountain range. If a name was unknown to me, I wanted to grow it, to see what it would turn into. And despite the inclemencies of a much lower and winter-wet habitat, I tried to make plants at home by providing them with a site, a soil, as much as possible like what they were used to. It was a way of compensating them for bringing so much of a world I would never get to on my own. And it meant that, finally, I had no pressing need to travel. The presences around me were more than sufficient to keep me fully aware and fully occupied. Perhaps Maeterlinck had it right after all. One can travel in one's own backyard.

IMPROBABLE JOURNEYS

Voyage Noir: Cuba, Haiti, Jamaica
1958

CUBA

After graduating from college in June 1958, I decided to accept Baudelaire's invitation and make a *voyage noir* of my own to a black republic—Haiti. A would-be poet, I was interested in possession, and in a country that featured a religion of possession—voodoo—there seemed much I could learn. Add the thrill of the name *Haiti,* only a twist of the alphabet from *Hades,* and a poverty ranked second to none, and there were reasons enough for a sheltered American to journey to the world's "best living nightmare."

When my Cuban cousins, Merrill and Alicia Matzinger, heard about my proposed trip, they insisted I make a ten-day detour to their suburban Havana home. There too, they said, was a Caribbean life I should see. I agreed, thinking of Cuba as a place to acclimatize and acquire the tropical vocabulary I needed for what lay ahead.

My cousins could not be there to entertain me, but they had arranged to have me taken out my first night by the Merrill Lynch branch manager, Chuck Tomkins, and his wife. Tomkins was no ordinary office manager. While working during the war for the CIA's predecessor, the Office of Strategic Services, he had been in charge of a dummy Merrill Lynch office in Santiago, Chile. That had given him a taste for the business and he continued with Merrill Lynch after the war. But by no means had he dropped the secret connection. My brother remembers Tomkins as one of a small group of business-suited types who regularly convened at the cellar safe house of our New York home, which my father had put at the CIA's disposal.

When we met at the Tomkins's house to get acquainted, it was only predictable that I should ask Chuck about the Castro insurgency I had read about in the *New York Times*.

At the mention of Castro, Tomkins bristled. "Castro may have a handful of outlaws hiding out with him in the Sierra Maestre. But the revolution you're asking about is nothing more than a figment of Stanley Mathews's imagination. Go anywhere and I bet you won't see anything that even begins to look like a revolution."

To show me what life in Havana was about at its best, the Tomkinses took me out for dinner to their friend Traficante's celebrated casino. As we came into the bar, I remember Chuck's introducing me to the ex-Chicago mobster, a handsome man's man in the chisel-featured Sinatra mold. Shaking my hand warmly, Traficante offered me the elegant drink there, a scotch and soda. Highball in hand, I drifted into the great gaming room. At that early hour it was patronized mainly by elderly dowagers, their long cubelike faces done up in accents of mascara and powder; a look, I felt, chosen to bring luck to their dice.

After dinner we sauntered to an outer patio to watch the dancing. The rumbas consisted of a single flute-sustained melodic line, repeated in varying intensities until, inexplicably, the piece came to a halt and the dancers sat down, becalmed. The men were all in white gabardine and danced as if planted in their tracks, trunks gently quavering to whatever wisps of rhythm pulsed forth from the orchestra.

The women were something else. Superbly gotten up in tight-fitting gowns, they pirouetted about their men, hips swishing like great tropical leaves.

My cousins' house was itself almost worth the detour. Painted a delicious raspberry, it fell in a spiral of seven terraces down the side of the Almendares Gorge. In the pool at the bottom floated the gold-and-white blossoms of a frangipani tree. Now and then, there was a frog to be fished out. As I swam, troops of vultures flashed overhead, dipping down over the high garden walls and gliding out over the gorge. In a moment they were back, lower this time, eyeing me as a cabby might a prospective fare, obliging me to keep paddling. Finally, after a couple of lengths, I felt free enough to float, nostrils distended, drinking in the vanillalike aroma of the blossoms and the odor of the pool's unraked leaves.

Wherever I went there were vultures, standing out in their somber coloring. They seemed to be forever eating, or on the lookout for the next meal. And the meals were well attended, producing an impression of sociability and surprisingly good manners. Driving about, I would come upon great clusters of these naked-headed birds, all gathered to one side of the road. As I passed them, they would stop and rise courteously into the air.

Among these graces, I could find only one shortcoming—their flight. I expected them to soar as gracefully as their northern counterparts, gulls and eagles. Instead, theirs was a jerky veering flight, more like a motorboat, as if the tropical air were an element to which they had adapted with difficulty—and only after long consultations.

Among the friends deputized to entertain me was Alicia's father, a Cuban sugar king, who took me out for lunch at his club. A big man, dressed in the white *guayabera* that seemed the official business uniform, he told me he had perfected his life so that he need never step out of the clean, white, bugless world represented by his air-conditioned Cadillac, office, restaurant, and social club.

After lunch, he showed me his yacht. A mate led us down through a narrow hatch. With pride, he pointed out the Waring blender and the cabins for friends, his mistress, and servants.

Apparently they all stayed down there for as long as a week at a time without dreaming of going up on deck, or of dropping a fishing line overboard and chancing contact with another order of being.

When I did escape from the Matzingers' friends into the old blue-cobbled squares of downtown Havana, my exhilaration was short lived. I became what any twenty-one-year-old strolling about all by himself is—a mark. For what else could I be there but to fuck? Harpies were legion: perched on stoops, clucking or hissing from doorways, even grabbing hold of my sleeve as they tried, by main force, to yank me inside. If I was lucky enough to nab a passing cab, the same invitations recurred, only now from the driver, with his stack of brothel cards, his photos of nubile fifteen-year-olds.

There seemed an all too single-minded sameness to this harassment, as if girls were a currency on which the national economy depended. And we tourists contributed our own bit. Unable to sleep, I let myself be taken by a young married Cuban from Tomkins's office—a man of the Left who was sympathetic to Castro—on an all-night round of floor shows, jukeboxes, slot machines, until, by 5 A.M. of the second night, I was willing to put up with anything rather than spend another dratted night beside a nonworking air conditioner. So I plunked down my remaining pesos, the female machine blinked and emitted its one wee grunt as I came, and that was that.

As for the man deputized to give me this tour, by the second evening we had become friends. Yet it was he who, for reasons I will never understand, was killed in the bloodbath following Castro's takeover.

Women in Havana seemed happy enough to accept the male view of them as so many voluptuous bodies. They dressed emphatically, their taste running to close-fitting sheaths, white if possible, clothing designed to accentuate or expound their ample figures.

Despite this emphasis on sheer physique, I felt there was something missing. Cuban women are said to have beautiful eyes. Maybe, indoors. But in going out, they made sure their eyes were masked behind dark glasses. What I did see was a plasticity in which effects of mass triumphed over line as color does over light. Hence the masks of rouge: young faces mottled into a smoky tropical sunset.

Magnificent sight: a Cuban in her sheath walking along an avenue, hips undulating like palm fronds.

———

Tomkins was right in that Havana was outwardly normal. There were no bombs or guns popping off. But I couldn't help being struck by the oversized weaponry being lugged about. And the numbers involved in keeping the girls and the casinos operating were considerable. Beside some twenty thousand policemen, all in mustachios, there were another ten thousand in business suits, riding three to a car, abetted by an estimated twenty thousand informers.

To prepare myself for Haiti I wanted to learn about *bembe,* the Cuban version of voodoo. Everyone I asked kept directing me to La Roux, a young woman who apparently never wore anything but black and curated in the Ethnological Museum. When I met her there one afternoon, she was willing to talk, but said it had to be after work. Pinning her to an appointment took some doing. After a botched rendezvous and no end of phone calls, she finally agreed to meet me on my next-to-last day at her mother's. There, while waiting for her to descend, her mother proudly showed me several small, green-lit tropical landscapes, painted while La Roux was studying at New York's Art Students' League.

When La Roux came down, she took me into a formal drawing room. Then she went around bolting various doors. What was all this secrecy about? I wondered.

Reading me, she said, "You may wonder at these precautions. But first let me apologize for the runaround I've been giving you. Any idea what's behind it?" She looked at me intently.

"None," I said, "I assumed you're a busy lady."

"I am," she said, "but there's more to it. Because you're leaving, I'm going to take a chance and trust you. I want you to know I'm a Communist and the job I do at the museum is a front for my work in the Castro underground."

I hadn't realized that Castro's insurgency might be Communist inspired. "How long," I asked, "have you been a member of the party?"

"My lover was killed in Fidel's original July 22 raid on Batista's palace. That's why I'm always in black. We can't let the authorities think they can silence us by rubbing out our leaders. But it's getting worse all the time. This morning I witnessed the execution of one of our brothers by a police firing squad."

She was speaking clearly, but I kept feeling that it was only the concentration demanded by an unaccustomed English that was keeping her from breaking down. "You probably can't see," she went on, "the extent to which civil liberties have broken down. Even pregnant women are no longer respected. For people like me, the streets are no longer safe."

(In movie theaters a few months earlier, as I later learned, supposedly pregnant women had delivered themselves of the bombs tucked under their skirts.)

Much as I sympathized with La Roux, I did not see how she could carry on as an urban guerrilla and expect to maintain her civil rights. I was also troubled by the absence of a political program. True, "Freedom!" was a much-voiced rallying cry. But how it was to be used, other than by avenging yourself on those who had killed your friends, had not occurred to her.

In my naïveté I wanted the badges *left* and *right* to carry a program. But a person does not necessarily go underground out of reasoned conviction. La Roux, I think, was expressing loyalty to a dead lover. And, in expressing it, she was demonstrating another kind of freedom. I may shrink before a sentimental yoking of the private and the public. But I can weep for a courage not my own.

On my last day in Cuba, as a special send-off, Alicia's mother, Blanca, a resourceful woman who had supported herself as a journalist in Miami after her divorce, drove me to her birthplace in Matanzas, an hour away. It may have been the mood I was still in after seeing La Roux, but the drive along a road framed in overarching acacia trees conveyed a distinct melancholy. Was it, I wondered, something to do with the effort required of the short trees, their having to pull themselves up on their toes in order to touch over the road, exposing their roots in the process? But on getting out to examine them more closely, I saw that practically half of the trees were memorials, their trunks pasted over with red-and-white stickers bearing the names of the latest traffic fatalities.

While driving through the old residential quarter of Matanzas, Blanca pointed out the intricate designs of ironwork balconies. "It's like Chantilly lace," she said, her eyes twinkling with pride at the simile she had conjured up.

After lunch, we descended in a big open elevator to see the caves, which were said to be beautiful. "In the state you're in," Blanca said, "they'll cheer you up."

As we walked along, our guide pointed out various formations of orange rock, stalactites twisted into shapes almost recognizable. "Here," he said, flashing his lamp onto a jagged wall, "is the Elephant. Over there," pointing into the indecipherable beyond, "the Manger with the Three Wise Men."

Our heads reeling from the sulphurous stench, we stumbled along behind, trying to anticipate what shadowed formation he would illuminate next and what name he would give it. At the time, I was put off by this Latin need, as I saw it, to make chance formations spout an all too inevitable ventriloquese. But shouldn't I have applauded the stalactites for addressing us, against the odds, in accents not so markedly different from our own?

HAITI

After the oppressiveness of Batista's Havana, Haiti offered a welcome relief. On the plane, as we passed over the island of Gonave, I noticed the turquoise and jade of the surrounding waters; those "inks," as I wrote in my diary, "not permitted in the classroom." On landing, I was struck by the clothes: how becoming blue was on a black body; how white, which in Havana would be merely emphatic, became a sign of modesty or religious humility. At noon I walked filled by the odors of thyme and pimiento. The very air seemed an aphrodisiac.

The residential Port-au-Prince I walked in, with its bright clothes and squatting mango vendors and cobblestone streets that twisted up the hillsides like serpents, had the feel of a magical painting. Childlike and, if you had the nose for it, only a year after Papa Doc Duvalier's accession, a bit sinister. Just as it was not unusual in a Haitian painting to see a road wind up toward a house and emerge as the extension of the chimney, so the same primitive logic appeared in ordinary life. On my second afternoon, a mulatto was shot dead as he walked down the street a few yards from where I was staying. When questioned, the soldier responsible could give no reason for pulling the trigger. Shortly thereafter the court ruled it was the soldier's gun, not the soldier, that was at fault.

It took me a while to get used to a world where things were communicated in gestures rather than words. When vendors pestered me, my instinct was to tell them to scram: "*Vas-y!*" No, my landlady explained, that's what you say to a dog. Instead, I should make them a sign. *No thank you,* I learned, was conveyed by raising an outspread hand.

As my ears became more attuned, I noticed how each trade, like a dance, was identified by a distinct beat. Shoeshine boys, for instance, announced themselves by tapping three quick clicks on their boxes. There were visual indicators as well. You distinguished the vendors of empty bottles by their heads, shaved in the form of an oval. When people wanted something from me they hissed (the children meowed). I was surprised by how far the hiss carried (like the word *sex* pronounced in a crowded room).

It was clear that it was their country, not mine. Nowhere was the hostility more pronounced than in Port-au-Prince's downtown market. Hundreds of vendors squatted by their boxes of mangos, eyeing them enviously, and eyeing this white man just as enviously. I had the impression that were I to pass out all of a sudden—from the heat, the stench—it wouldn't be long before they had various chunks of me up for sale on a hundred different stands.

I was not used to the congestion, the sheer numbers of people hanging about, or the good humor with which, when taking a small bus, or *camionette,* they insisted on wedging themselves in, as close as possible to their neighbors. Should another come along, instead of throwing up their hands and protesting, they obligingly made room.

I invariably encountered them either in groups or sitting surrounded by merchandise. And I could never stroll past without having someone from the group call out and offer to accompany me wherever I was headed. So convinced were they of my great need—why else was I walking all alone?—they saw nothing amiss in charging me for the pleasure of their presence.

Yet a hanger-on, too, could have his pride. I remember a man who had taken me swimming to a distant mud beach happen-

ing to lose his comb in the murky water. For half an hour, up to
his knees, he thrashed about, trying to find it. He even made me
feel responsible for what had happened. But when I offered to
buy him another one—anything to leave!—he wouldn't hear of
it. Instead, he told me resourcefully, he would come back the
next day at low tide.

Of the five Haitian contacts given me, the first I looked up
was Hervé Télémaque, a painter of my age who had spent the
previous year studying at the Art Students' League in New York.
Hervé took one look at Mon Repos, where I was staying in central Port-au-Prince, and suggested I move up the mountain to a
pension in the mulatto suburb of Pétionville. There, every afternoon, on the pretext of paying court to the owner, one of the
first widows of the Duvalier regime, he would come and ask me
what I had noted during my day's wanderings. We soon found
we had a number of enthusiasms in common: poets like Henri
Michaux, who I was translating by the hotel poolside each afternoon, and painters like Larry Rivers, whose work he knew
from New York.

Born in another country, Hervé might have become something else besides a painter. But in Haiti, thanks to André Breton and the Centre d'Art's direct responsibility for the 1947 revolution, only a month after Breton's visit, painting had become
the major vehicle in forging a new national consciousness.
Hervé did not paint like a Haitian primitive, because he was not
a Haitian primitive. But he could bring a Haitian color sense
into modern painting, succeeding to the point where, in a few
years, he would become Europe's leading pop art painter.

When conversing with Hervé, I tried to respond pictorially.
If he characterized M., a poet who had turned to writing plays
in Creole, as a corrupted artist, I would try to imagine the color
of such corruption—a bright carmine? If he talked about the
obsession with death—for Haitians, the state of greatest actual-

ity—I would try to relate it to his own use of black to bring out and clarify other colors in his paintings.

When a poet or artist puts together an image world, the qualities he normally wants in it are clarity, fluency. Not Hervé! He prefers concepts, obsessions that are almost religious, such as *Africa, the Sea, the Mountain.* They are his lamps; he spreads them as a hunter would the strands of a net thrown out at night across a game trail. The image-concept, as it is caught, keeps trying to change into something else, the mountain becoming first an elephant, then a breast, then a mask, green.

Like most Haitians, he has seen the mountain move. It is that touch of lava he must bring to his work.

The colors Hervé knows: white (very well). It gives contrast, density. Black, but black more as a medium than a color. It provides background, relief. Green, a bright tropical green. Later, a darker, more raucous green will emerge, a green like the green in *verde* that croaks and conveys envy and jealousy.

Yellow, to be sure, but yellow is more problematic and has to be used sparingly, to outline, say, the rich triangle of a woman's sex. For joy, he prefers a milky blue that he associates with a faraway time, a pool with white breasts or the sea emerging with a fringe of sail at the upper edge of his insular consciousness.

Hervé introduced me to some musician friends. They took me to the single voodoo rite I was to see, a minor ritual thanking the gods for a ceremony that had been concluded successfully the previous evening.

The excitement I had missed could be inferred from the elaborate visual invitations to the gods chalked on the temple floor, the offerings of rum and *clairin,* and the sexy dancing of the head priest. But that made the ceremony all the more frustrating since everyone, from the drummers on down, seemed to be taking things pretty casually. There was general consternation when, despite everything, two white-garbed women keeled over and had to be brought round and led outside. It wasn't, on this night at least, called for.

The dancing drew on an array of gestures—nervous, staccato, and made all the more so by the butting in, over two drums, of the big *maman* drum with its own imperious demands. And, throughout it all, the twitching of shoulders—like someone showing you the whites of his eyes.

Possession is the product of self-hypnosis brought on by the repetitiveness of dancing in place when combined with everything else assailing the senses. But ultimately it's the spinal cord that is taking the drubbing. In the course of being pulled, jarred by such conflicting beats, an unknown self can come to the fore, the person one can be only in those conflicted circumstances. And while the possessing force, the *lwa* as they call it, varies from person to person, it is absolutely visceral. At the moment of impact one comes.

The day after the ceremony I called on Titon, a tall, strikingly handsome "man of the people" who would star in Maya Deren's *Divine Horsemen,* a great documentary about voodoo and the life it involves. Everything about Titon evinced style: from the way in which, on greeting a woman dancer, he would lurch back and shake his hips in acknowledgment, to the elegance with which he disposed of a half-smoked cigarette, laying it butt end out over the window sill of his newly purchased thirty-five-dollar cabin.

As he was taking me around several temple sites, I asked Titon why there was so little voodoo to be seen. That was because, he replied, all the voodooists were at Saut d'Eau–Ville Bonheur in the hilly interior for the great pilgrimage of the Haitian year. He would be there, Titon said, if he hadn't used up his funds buying his shack. So I suggested we both go and I would pay his expenses.

When I showed up next morning, I found his brother waiting as well, whose fare I was expected to pay. There was also a small satchel containing Titon's three shirts, an extra pair of trousers, and his dancing boots. Why he felt obliged to take his whole wardrobe I don't know, but it made me, in my fifties garb of khaki pants and sneakers, feel rather underdressed.

Our bus was a converted truck. For much of an hour we drove about, shouting directions and luring in whomever we could, until the benches were all filled, seven or eight to a row. Not even in the subway had I ever experienced anything like the bus's compacted sensuality: the smells, the bare backs, the differently glowing skins. Directly in front was a young mother with beautiful eyes, not the clouded ones I so often saw, who rode most of the way with her right hand elegantly resting on her shoulder—was there no other space? While we waited for the bus to fill, Titon gently massaged her back. The women rode up front, the men in the rear. Not far from me was a pint-sized Tonton Macoute in the already notorious dark glasses, who kept demanding quaffs from the bottle of rum tucked under our shoes. To make sure we got the point, he showed his loaded holster: "If you have any trouble in Saut d'Eau . . ."

As we were getting under way, a man with a banjo clambered aboard. To my delight, he launched into a medley of merengue dance tunes right out of the ten-inch Harold Courlander LP that had nourished me through college. But this was not a carnival outing and, before we were even out of the suburbs, the banjo music had given way to the Carmelite hymn they would sing some twenty times before we arrived. Soon Titon was in full throat himself, leading them in the chorus in a rasping cigarette-laced voice. And, after a number of hymns, he broke in and intoned a priestly novena. I was, to say the least, startled.

The countryside seemed densely inhabited, with crops sprinkled haphazardly about the hilly terrain. But the plots were rarely bigger than the size of a room and looked hardly capable of feeding one of us, let alone a family. But what worried Titon when we passed a band of ragged beggar children with horribly bloated bellies was the likelihood that they might never have been baptized. He and a friend argued over it for the next fifteen minutes.

It was midafternoon when we finally arrived in Ville Bonheur, a town only an hour and a half away by normal car. At Titon's suggestion we hired horses from a crone and, with her behind us, set off for Saut d'Eau and its sacred waterfall some four miles away. The sight of Titon saying "*salope*" to his nag as he urged him on, and of me being able to make mine trot only with the help of the crone running behind with her switch, had everyone we passed convulsed in stitches.

On the hilltop overlooking the waterfall, I found some friends sprawled out with a picnic hamper. After satisfying my hunger, I changed into a bathing suit and slid on my ass down the mud slope. I arrived in time to see a woman in the throes of possession being helped across the lower part of the waterfall. She appeared to be trying to crab walk on her back, while guttural moans escaped from her. The force of the three-hundred-foot fall on the top of my skull was certainly dizzying, and I could see it triggering a fit of possession.

The waterfall was full of thousands of laughing, half-naked celebrants. There were even cast-off bathing suits to be seen floating joyfully downstream.

Emerging from the bottom of the cataract, I found myself among a bunch of carts drawn up to a candle-covered tree sacred to the snake god, Damballah. Among them were vendors selling pop and what must have been marijuana. But since the crone was waiting with our two horses halfway up the slope there was no way of indulging myself.

My friends had no intention of making a night of it. But they kindly looked up a painter friend, who offered me a bed with a *fille,* apparently the only combination available, for seventy-five cents. Like an idiot I turned it and the rest of the night's entertainment down in the hope that, by staying with Titon, I might run into some voodoo. After all, that's what I had come for.

The rest of the day could not have been more disastrous. Much of it we spent wandering about in the rain looking for a place to sleep. Renting a hut for a dollar was easy compared to finding the requisite bedding. For the better part of an hour I remained concealed in the shadows while Titon bargained for a rush mat. After probing it for lice, as if they were something I could see, we repaired to a cooking hut manned by a pal of Titon for a restorative coffee. But the coffee came too late for Titon, and in the midst of an unholy downpour he fell asleep.

With no idea how to find the little hut we had rented, I had no choice but to try to wake him by tugging at his boots. Finally, after a half hour of being poked, he steered me out through the slippery mud. Titon himself took up most of the bed and the whole of the sheet, while I lay on what was left of the mat listening enviously to the music blaring forth from the dance huts. I slept fitfully, prey to a series of nightmares and, in the early morning, dreams in which I saw Titon awake. But each time I checked him out there he was sound asleep. By then it was time for the six roosters huddled under our bed to start crowing. Unable to take any more, I went off to try to have breakfast, buying a bowl of soup and selling it back, a mouthful later, at half price.

But the roosters had given Titon ideas. After selling our mat, he invested the proceeds in a chicken to take back to what he called a bit grandly his ménage, the five pals with whom he somehow shared his one-room house.

By now it was time for the pilgrimage's concluding rite, a formal mass in a huge sun-blazed square. Through it all the jammed throng showed no animation until it was time for the Carmelite hymn. The night before, Titon had taken me through the square aglow with several thousand pilgrim candles and had me buy him a song book. With the whole square as their chorus, Titon and the priest sang, virtually alone, all twenty-two verses.

From our hired bus we watched the final procession, everyone solemnly, sensuously, trailing the priest who was singing once again the hymn. "*Magnifique,*" Titon called it. Indeed!

It took us several hours to round up a sufficient complement of passengers to fill the bus. And because the driver had a slow-moving vehicle, he refused to let passengers make their usual stops for roast corn, a drink of pop, whatever. Finally, in response to the growing volume of protests, he pulled up by a brook in open countryside. We all piled out, the women squatting gracefully in their skirts a few feet from the highway, the men wandering about like goats.

The next day, when I told the renowned voodoo authority Milo Rigaud about our fiasco, he called Titon an *esprit frivole.* That was why he had never been elevated to full voodoo priest, as might have been expected of one of his gifts. A premature judgment. Before dying at thirty-one—could AIDS have existed that early?—Titon did become a *houngan,* apparently a good one. And I have never passed a movie poster of him as a young man dancing in the throes of possession without bursting into tears. Perhaps it was only in front of the camera that he generated this charisma, but it remains deeply impressive.

JAMAICA

With a week to spare before I had to be back in New York, I took a flight to Kingston. The town struck me as a version of an American inner city, dirty and more than a little dangerous. The streets were so full of pimps that it took a certain concentration just to keep walking. Then on street corners, as I hesitated to ponder a direction, the most improbable washerwomen would blossom forth as prostitutes, insisting with an earnestness that made my skin crawl.

With no thought other than of removing myself I caught a train to Montego Bay, at the other end of the big island. We were hardly out of the city when the train ground to a sudden halt in the middle of an abandoned rye field. I asked the pretty Chinese teenager sitting opposite, a big packet of piano sheet music bulging from her lap, what had happened. "There's been an accident," she explained. Apparently a man accused of arson had strapped himself to the track as a way of protesting his innocence and the conductor had managed to halt the train in the nick of time. As we waited for the man to be led away, an argument broke out in the seat behind me over the meaning of *arson*. One man stoutly maintained it meant suicide. And he refused to yield, insisting that from the point of view of a functioning society, an arsonist condemned to a long-term sentence might as well have committed suicide.

With the conversational wheels now oiled, the Chinese girl and I embarked on a discussion of female beauty. We were seemingly agreed on most of the particulars when I made the mistake of commenting favorably on a woman in a tomato-red skirt seated at the far end of our carriage. "Why, she's black!" the girl almost shrieked.

She got off at Mandalay. Soon thereafter, the train entered a lush mountain rain forest that had us all riding with our heads out the windows like dogs. At the stations women vendors appeared with trays of delicious tiny bananas. The journey began to look as if it could be going somewhere.

I had been supplied with a four-page list of hotels, but nothing under six dollars. Taking advantage of the camaraderie that built up, I asked a hillsman if he knew of anything cheaper. He obliged by writing down an address that turned out to be a rather dear one-block taxi ride from the station. The large, thickset proprietress who greeted me in the somewhat seedy hall must have been part Indian, with a great mane of yaklike hair flowing down her back. But the room was clean, with a wash pail in the corner and a daddy longlegs keeping order over the bed, while the view gave onto a gas station dominated by a huge rock-and-roll jukebox.

After a nap I went out to grab a bite. The first person I accosted, a giant policeman in a red-and-purple-striped uniform, looked me up and down and asked where I was staying. When I told him, he burst into a delicious chuckle. Taking me by the shoulder, he then steered me to a restaurant two blocks away that sported a bar and a small dollar-a-night hotel upstairs. From then on I was pretty much set.

I asked the cab driver dining beside me where I could find calypso. I had been enthralled by the music from the age of fourteen, when I had come upon an Edmundo Ros dance record that belonged to my parents. There are other forms of popular music from the same era that speak to me more now: the jigs and heartrending waltzes of Cajun music, the anecdotes of loss that in Hank Williams spiral to a tragic poetry. But calypso was a sexual celebration that, like "Rum and Coconut Water," was not easily come by in fifties America. And the dialect, with its last syllable accentuation and softened speech, could produce off-color lyrics of a delicious ambiguity:

> *Kitch, come home to bed*
> *I got a small comb*
> *To scratch your head*
> *Kitch, don't make me sigh*
> *You know I love you*
> *You're playing shy*

But was it "shy," or as my ears jubilantly wanted it, "you play inside"? The cab driver directed me to the promisingly named

Needle's Eye, a cathouse of the sort that must have been legion in pre-1917 New Orleans. A big rickety wooden staircase led me past an outdoor bar and into the dance hall, empty except for a few prostitutes huddled by the jukebox. From behind an American-style bandstand a large fan blew aimlessly. The girls were all dressed in single-color one-shoulder-tied evening dresses, a sash accentuating their waists, and their hair piled in a thick bun off the back of their heads. In an hour or so the jitterbugging would begin, the girls sashaying in tight, intricate steps taken at double time.

While waiting on the balcony for the calypso to get under way, I found myself joined by a part-Chinese prostitute, Cynthia. With some awe, I had been watching her patiently counting an impressive wad of bills. She was dressed in a shiny green gown with a deep décolleté, the vee extending just below her breasts. When I expressed my pleasure in it, she informed me proudly that she had made it herself. One day she hoped to go to New York and work for a dress designer.

In the course of trying to make conversation I asked if she had ever wanted to get married, a sally greeted with a contemptuous snort.

"But you must have a steady man, a pimp," I said, feeling my way.

"No," Cynthia replied, "I've never had a pimp."

Impressed by her wad—more than enough to get her to New York—I continued to press. "Haven't you ever paid a man to sleep with you?"

"Sure I have. I even kept one fellow for several months. But for people like us, it's not a good practice."

While we chatted, the Friday night crowd drifted in, workers with more cash than they could see themselves taking home to their wives. Finally, when the movie house next door let out, calypso began. The songs were chanted by the Calypsonian, a figure in florid shirt and straw hat, flourishing maracas as his badge of office. Backing him up was a guitarist, a bassist twanging a giant one-note box, and a pint-sized drummer who, between choruses, footed it with white female tourists.

When the band retired, the whores took over, singing folk songs and the local *mente,* an agricultural calypso. In the dance hall inside, couples perspired against the red glow of the jukebox, the girls' hair unpinned and cascading in buckets as they jitterbugged with the short broken strokes of skaters, catching the beat farther and farther back on their heels, faces in a melting orange-blue light, hair flowing in an ease of water over a hydroelectric dam.

Persian Mirages
1962, 1967

In the 1960s, Persia could often seem a land of mirages, more an abstract idea than a country with actual borders and a homogeneous character. Anyone meeting a Persian at the time might not be amiss in supposing that this remote "Iran" of deserts and mountains, with its few people and no women (none with unveiled faces)—where to travel at all required both a dust mask and a spare intestine—was arbitrarily created on a whim by the folks at Rand McNally. What kept it going over millennia may turn out to have been nothing more than a language and, even more unlikely, a body of great poetry.

In the face of hazards, I do what I can. I visit the principal cities, all quite modern—their predecessors had been razed again and again—and the five or six surviving world-class monuments. I find a friend who has a car. With his help, something of the old Persia that inspired the Alhambra, that still glimmers in any number of museum collections and old travel accounts, comes through: a roadside mosque, its blue dome encircled by wind; a garden with battered mud walls and an overgrown pergola in whose shade you can stroll, with no one pointing at your blond unveiled wife, where there are trees, a couple of maples, the sound of water (seen water distracts, especially when filled with goldfish or lilies)—and flowers that, for once, do more than spell out a name, a cause. For the traveler, that may be more than enough. A stray scent has gotten through, miraculously preserved.

From my first six-week stay I returned home, relatively satisfied, until a friend asked if couldn't I have seen more of the Persia I sought by spending a couple of hours at the local museum. It was the one that had first prompted my notion of visiting the people generally credited with inventing our word *paradise*. That made me remember how another writer had portrayed them, as a people so enamored of beauty as to be virtually helpless before anything possessing it—a horse or a twelve-year-old boy.

To oblige my friend, I go with him to the museum. We find ourselves standing before a case of twelfth-century lusterware. A number of pots clash hopelessly, jumbled one against another. Then I spot it, a pot with a blue, almost violet, ground, intense as the Persian sky. On it the painter has brushed a face round and smiling, a face like a bell whose black curves move outward against the rim until they seem entirely to fill it—like a peach tree encountered at the end of a long flower-lit pool. It stands there in its arch, blossoms perfectly still, like a friend who comes and with his smile completes your happiness.

GARDENS

"Beauty," Wallace Stevens wrote, "is momentary in the mind," and often in Persia it is more the idea of the garden that impresses than anything leafed out in bald mud pathways and cypresses. Travelers who come looking for a garden listed on the municipality's tourist map may find nothing there, the whole arbor having dried up like the famous river outside Shiraz. Like oil, a garden is perhaps not a thing to be seen so much as to be divined, an invitation of leaves extending over high mud walls.

Still searching for a garden, you sign up for a tour that promises to take you through the whole of the city. (If its main street is the Four Gardens, there must be one or two lurking somewhere?) Well, you are wrong, there is only a pair of shaking minarets giving onto distant grape-colored mosques and some storks nesting amid the domes of a nearby slum.

But you have come too far to give up. Climbing into a taxi, you mutter another garden name. Fifteen minutes later, the driver pulls up before the usual barrier of mud and stones. There, while he waits, a gate opens and you go into a modest pergola strewn with vine leaves and unopened wisteria, where a lone student, book in hand, walks, memorizing his required verses. Other features come into view: banks of grass into which pansies have been sown with a richness that affronts at first, but which one ends by accepting, as one accepts an old lady's jewels; little five-sided pools bordered on one side by a screen of cypresses and, on the other, by a bleak terrace where a volley of crows sits feasting, their color a jangle of gray and gold in the luminous March air.

The remainder presents a crazy quilt of quince, plum, peach, cherry, pear, pistachio. Maidenly ash trees rise all white to a considerable height, when suddenly, like a skirt poised over the head, a hoop of green appears. And, blossoming everywhere, the red-budded extravagance of the Judas tree. All this is jumbled pell-mell to create a sense of profusion, of all nature being there, contained—in a word, plenitude.

Even shade has to be constructed. The gardener makes a bower of a group of maples planted in a circle, or a long rectangle if there is space. He then laces the bower with the burble of water flowing in perpetual conversation. The banks he dresses with an ebullience of narcissi and fat-mouthed irises. If then a pair of nightingales can be induced to nest in the adjoining shrubbery, his delight knows no bounds. You see him sitting with maybe a pot of tea set on a silver tray and, on a little carpet, heaped-up bowls of oranges and black dates. These he will serve you himself, smiling even though never having met you before, knowing no words will do in place of a smile.

In a world where everything must be built of mud and smacks of impermanence, little survives that has not been willed. Tomorrow perhaps there will be an earthquake, or a government seizure. And the gardens, you come to feel, sense all this. Nothing would suit them better than to be turned into carpets: the carpet the religious man mounts in the same spirit with which a more secular Persian steps into a car to head out into a highway that he sees as a vast undulating lake, all breath, stars, and the ultimate tinkle of shattering glass.

MOMENTS

In a world of such fragility one impulse may be to flee, and many ambitious Persians have gone abroad. Once they are established there, it is hard to entice them back to a daily round of intrigue, constant hypocrisy, and endless, endless cups of tea. One would not be far off the mark in suspecting that, without all the tea, nothing would ever be transacted, nor would there be any officials left on their feet. Yet the same annoyances that render any decision making so frustrating also enable the private individual to turn himself out like a carpet for a friend.

At home, the private man surrounds himself in a rind of abstractions that make up a music without beginning, middle, or end, because it is essentially without hope. Yet the more accustomed to this music you become, the more it seems to take on the colors of thought itself, of that grief in which Rilke saw the source of any truly meditative poetry.

Unable to believe in a prospective future, without even a verb tense to express such a notion (in Persian, one doesn't say "I shall," but a more realistic "I wish to"), he must try to sustain himself in a present as magically continuous as one of those endless flower-studded meadows in which the prince of a Persian miniature sits. As we see him there, face unlined like a child's, he is happy, sated, very near sleep. But unlike his Western counterpart, who exists only in his anticipation—and must realize it all over a three-martini lunch break—everything that surrounds him, the courtiers under a distant peach tree tuning their lutes, the girl dandling like a ripe bough in his lap, ensures that he will wake and wander forth down one of those long vistas. There perhaps on another page we will see him, lost in the silence of all that grows, while all around him the blossoms fall, their poignant notes distinct as crystals. Under their spell he has become once again a toddler, drunk on his first legs, for whom the sky's blue is hope itself.

The Persian sky is much of the time so near, as it settles onto its frame of bare, mustard-colored hills, that anyone must feel he can reach up with his hands and touch it, mouth bursting in a great podlike grin.

PERSEPOLIS

Abstractions succeed as private, miniature creations. For the traveler who insists on something larger, there is Persepolis, a structure that dwarfs even palace grounds of the Versailles type that were built to be viewed from a horse.

Approaching Persepolis, the vast surroundings look outsized, made up of greenish-yellow hills that stretch into the lowering sky like shaggy camels, sky and hills being so much the same in tone that it is impossible to tell where one leaves off and the other begins. Nearing it, the haze thickens. The plain looks infinite. Then the palace bursts upon you, great columns looming from inflated platforms like the one and only palace of the one and only kingdom.

It is the palace's situation, at the top of the once very fertile plain of Marvdasht, that impresses. All the rest—glossy friezes with processions of tireless Medes and Persians trooping up the same stairs, great portals on which the same imperial lion, facial muscles contorted, is always ravaging the same donkey—can seem, several millennia later, invidious propaganda. The gestures are so stylized the spectator feels shut out, repelled, and, if he allows himself to be so, humbled. Persians though, have gotten over this and, in a shrunken dominion, have created a culture that relishes its own momentariness—a cry, into the unspeakable night, rising.

TEHRAN

The hub of modern Persia is Tehran. In all respects a creation of the Turkish-speaking Qajar dynasty who came from nearby, it has grown from a few thousand in the early nineteenth century to a city of over two million in the midtwentieth.

Of early Tehran, little survives beyond the bazaar and the Khake Golistan royal palace with its famous peacock throne. Picture a pastry-tiled chateau decorated with much cut glass and a series of large golden peacock clocks still bearing their original advertisements: "This superb piece of machinery was made by Thomas Byrne near the King's palace, 50 St. James Street." Napoleon had sent the bearded Qajar a set of Sèvres porcelain depicting his campaigns, while the czar contributed a cheesy sword set with small turquoises. It seems clear what they thought of him. The visitor's interest is drawn more by the carpet-strewn floors, the gleaming winter garden with its rows of tufted plane trees, or the lateral facades where desultory repairs are being carried out under the eyes of two bayonet-wielding guardsmen.

A taxi ride back through the modern town fails to reveal much besides neo-Parthian government architecture and the occasional business-suited or veiled Tehrani. On curbstones, sunburned men sit polishing oranges with pink nylon toothbrushes. Perhaps a tall gaunt vendor wearing a cap on his shaved crown may emerge from the traffic pushing an equally tall narrow wagon filled with pots of long-stemmed carnations. Along an open gutter, a few women squat happily, sipping the water as they wash their hands. Farther along, on a patch of sun-warmed rotary, men in overalls and yellow caps snooze facedown, oblivious of the swirling traffic and the figure in red shirt and white-handkerchief-wrapped head streaking by on a purple bicycle.

The traffic is of a striking virulence. There is not a car that isn't in some way scratched or dented.

One sympathizes with a former premier who levied an import tax on cars as an unaffordable luxury. Since for the Tehrani a car has magical properties, there was no collecting the tax, and the premier was himself dismissed. Each year the legislature delegates a good part of its oil revenue to highway construction. But an instinct for self-preservation makes sure that few highway projects pass beyond an initial road surfacing. Funds are diverted, and every couple of months members of the cabinet are rumored to be at the airport, on their way to join erstwhile colleagues in Zurich or Long Beach.

Few car owners risk doing their own driving. Safer to hire a fellow newly arrived from the country, in the same spirit that, a hundred years ago, an army draftee might hire a peasant to take his place. The chauffeur, in turn, hires someone with a suit and dark pointed shoes and perhaps a flower over his left ear to sit beside him, ready whenever they bang into something to leap out and gesticulate.

With all the chauffeurs and their friends and the workers hired for nonexistent construction projects, Tehran's population has more than doubled since the Second World War. Fortunately, the city's ravines have encouraged the construction of overlapping one-story houses, without the high-rise's visual affront. For the more well-to-do, modern architecture offers its particular refinements. Thus, houses have no windows, or the merest slit such as one finds in medieval towers, through which the day's weather (dust, snow) may be reckoned. And gardens are all of the walled compound variety. When asking why, one is told, "Thieves." Against creatures whose resourcefulness rivals that of Zeus, precautions can never be too elaborate.

THE CHADOR

A more personal wall is the chador, a black veil that utterly encloses every woman from nose to toe. Unlike vaguely similar equipment, such as the raincoat or muumuu, the chador is primarily for the face. On busy streets, women with a baby in each arm secure their chadors by holding them between clenched teeth. The need to cover the face is so much a part of a woman's modesty that, should you blunder upon a lady taking a bath in the courtyard, she will instinctively grab a towel and wrap it around her face. Blindfolded thus, but her essential modesty preserved, she will stand there carrying on the usual exchange of amenities until a servant arrives to shoo you out.

A code so adhered to is not easily given up, no matter how many royal edicts are issued. In Tehran at midcentury, a number of emancipated women did not wear the chador. But few would think of going out without covering their faces in a thick glaze of red powder that is almost as effective. Yet the chador is far from brick solid. It can be adjusted to the needs of a moment, much as when a Western woman with attractive legs fidgets with her skirt to call attention to all that lies under it.

THE CULT OF GARDENS

At the end of much dust the Persian city appears, in a greeting, an explosion of trees. It is the encircling belt of green that gives a city its feeling of a garden. The city itself is more a maze of rectangular mud-baked dwellings and crisscrossing powder-white streets that wind on and on like the tunneled castles children build to roll marbles down: a jigsaw puzzle of holes and sudden luminous squares over which the blue of a mosque dome plays, much as fountains play in Italy.

To inhabitants of the desert the city is paradise—a walled place within which things grow. Since rain is far from common, the matter of growth may be illusory. (In Shiraz, *the* garden city, it hadn't rained in three years.) Yet city dwellers believe in it and, in acting upon it, they transform the city into a place where they and their desires meet.

Much civic revenue goes into the planting of trees and flower-clock rotaries. Shops announce themselves with baskets of flowers and display their wares as if they were blossoms. Should an actual garden exist—even if so remote as to be essentially unvisitable—it becomes a source of civic pride. Newspapers follow its seasonal progress with an avidity reserved elsewhere for the local ball team. The plot need not even be very large. In Yazd, the east gate garden took the form of a rotary dominated by a statue of the Shah's father. At sundown, half the town convened to observe the floral display—as New Yorkers might the skaters in Rockefeller Center—while traffic caromed around and the near mountains glowed.

Should your city not possess a garden, you do not let that discourage you. Soon enough, one of numerous holidays will provide an occasion to set out with your friends (the women, of course, in the rear, bearing quilts and hand stoves) for a plantation at the perimeter, where a shriveled stream with its couple of scraggly willows is all that remains of the bountiful river by which Sa'dī picnicked.

HUCK FINNS

In the spectrum of gardens the ne plus ultra is composed of nothing but water itself, a flowerless, white, splashing roar. There were several such north of Tehran, where business-suited men came to lunch like Huck Finns on wooden rafts riveted in mid-torrent. The scene was such that we walked for a while, clambering ibexlike over a landscape of little waterfalls and pink knobbly mountains right out of a miniature, while below us men in blue pants and marigold shirts, coats off and heads in each other's laps, lolled on carpeted rafts among mounds of watermelon, orange pop, and fried chicken.

As we crossed overhead on a footbridge, diners would reach up a handful of pistachios. Farther upstream, strollers swayed under carpets and melons. Traversing the slippery logs and stones was difficult until we realized we wouldn't fall, that the logs only constituted an illusion of peril, like a fun-house tunnel.

Eventually, we took up a place on one of the rafts. Shirt whites dazzled nearby, set against thick eyebrows and blue-black hair, against the turquoise of a bridge railing. In the midst of so much roaring water, I felt suspended—a crow, wings spread, floating between trees—as if it were not a raft I was on, but a tree house, the kind into which a child climbs to rocket off into his own white, annihilating ascent.

ASCENSIONS

This yearning, encountered everywhere, comes from a world where protective hedges really are of mud; where the unrolling of a carpet, or the soft underhanded gesture of a mason tossing bricks, seem at one with bubble-domed houses. What keeps it from giddy Platonism is a respect for human momentariness. No one would want to rocket away if he thought he would have to soar there all day like a vulture.

Here color is like Jack's beanstalk. To the wish to ascend it brings sudden speed, but at the same time it identifies property and keeps it from disappearing. Bicycles are painted a visible red or purple, lampposts a startling yellow, railings turquoise. Enter a taxi, and you enter a swirl of plastic flowers, dangling dolls, and belly-dancer photos, all jangling together against fake zebra seat covers. The color may be inspired by water-pipe visions. But it is also the city dweller's reaction to the gray monotony of the surrounding dustscape.

In a rug, the sensuality of certain dyes provides all the magic needed to float away. Often enough, they are colors that your own eye might not respond to. In a warehouse courtyard, among hundreds of carpets, someone may suddenly exclaim about what seems the most humdrum of prayer carpets, a rose-madder ground outlined in blue. But as you gaze, you find yourself riveted by an earth pink that has started to glow, to spread, like the freshest of dawn juices.

With such vivacity, spatial relations change, and a Westerner strolling in the bazaar can come away numbed by the head-jerking zigzags of suspended articles: pots, scarves, towels, vests, and bed linens. Because tots are not pushed about on strollers, but carried high, propped on a brother's shoulders, they are one with the hanging phantasmagoria of household decoration. In a patio, the only grounded plants are grass and pansies. The rest present a hanging stream of color in which you move, bathed by sudden flashes. When a householder waters, it is not the ground, but the walls, the patio air, he mists. He does it, he says, to cool the house for sleeping. But when the time comes, he goes off to the still cooler roof.

For those more socially inclined, the high cracked sidewalks serve something of the function of a balcony. You go there to sit, to talk, to observe the traffic or take a nap, and you would no more think of walking on one than you would think of walking on a friend's dining room table.

SKY

Above the elements of earth and water comes sky. In a mosque, the levels are not tied to earth, but float in the upward thrust of the petitioner's hands. One honeycombed arch after another projects out, only to be caught by the next concealed band of brick.

But the sky of the dome is a tile mixed with mud, with you. Its patterns demonstrate how you can extricate yourself, climb a flowering lattice of color, and soar away. At the top, night itself, the lost boundaries of algebra.

DINING

You eat with spoon and fork, using the fork also as a pusher. In restaurants the utensils arrive in a large glass of water which is described as "boiling." They are often sent back.

The napkins—bits of colored tissue paper—repose in a second glass. A carbonated water drink, *abdugh,* may also be on the table. As you take a seat, mint leaves arrive to refresh you. You eat them squashed in a flap of bread; or, if thirsty, you swallow them plain. With everything, salt of course. You find it mixed into yogurt and sprinkled on cherries. After the last courses of fruit and jam, tea arrives, served in a tiny glass on a saucer. You drink it with several lumps of sugar—the biggest are reserved for guests— holding the sugar between your teeth and using tea as a chaser. Rather than wait for the tea to cool, most drink it out of the saucer little by little, sloshing it around and adding sugar to taste.

Others lounge about, inhaling huge water pipes. Maybe a friend sits near for comfort, but there is no chatting between them. After a while, dizzy, but pacified by inward concentration, they stagger to their feet like turtles surfacing.

Time now for a nap. And you see them sprawled, fists

clenched, on the raised, maybe eight-inch-wide, outer ledge of a shop. Or even upright, like one huge shopkeeper, bulging arms twined around an equally mammoth cash register. Others, more agile, squat over their heels, gradually reducing themselves to a needle point, a fleck of dust in the great desert of existence.

DRESS

To the city dweller dress is important, and it is carried off with an éclat that would make an Italian's eyes water. From the sneaker-shod, white-robed mullahs—always encountered hugging walls—to the man in a homemade suit of blue-and-gray stripes accompanied by a tie of the same startling cloth, to the hotel clerks in their 1880-style waistcoats (with high-nipped waist and plunging neck), a definite style is apparent. A uniform not only is satisfying but also often leaves the wearer dazed, able to do little more than stand before a hall mirror, lost in quiet admiration. At any hour you may find an entire hotel staff napping on a great length of carpet. But as soon as you pass, they spring to their feet and begin combing themselves, brushing off each other's coats and trousers.

The higher you ascend in the social hierarchy, the more important tailoring becomes. If you are a suppliant who wants a ministerial favor, you are shown into a small waiting room, and there you sit while the minister makes himself ready. The last silver lock in place (you glimpse the final touches as the secretary draws back the door), he receives you, a sweet smile conveying how happy he is to be speaking French—his syllables practically purr! You quickly understand the strains your request would impose on an overburdened staff. But you come away admiring his blue suit, batiste shirt, and flowing tie; that air, so wonderfully maintained, of a large refined mouse.

Character comes in the form of an exuberantly tortured crag

of a nose over which eyebrows jut like fierce rainbows. Unfortunately, some great noses can evoke mirth. Those needing to inspire fear, such as truck drivers, take care to flourish thick bushy moustaches; nothing to detract from the pool-like menace of the eyes. And it is the eyes, along with their night-colored hair, that gives avenue strollers the look of fantastically elegant, sad crows.

Hairstyles may range from flat in the middle, with the sides swept back in ram's horns, to a carefully combed crest, as expressive as the back of a pair of hands as it flops in conversation.

In more traditional milieus, turbans take over: green, if the wearer is a descendant of Muhammad; otherwise yellow, white, or a sprightly plaid. Some especially formal ones remind you of soap bubbles that would collapse if you blew hard. When all this appears on a wide tree-lined avenue at 5 P.M., the effect can be quite startling—a whole avenue reeking of attar of rose!

WOMEN

Women, those black blurs going by on the street, are essentially invisible. Yet if at all like the little girls in the bazaar, they may be the most brilliant creatures going. Alas, those "wild black eyes" zip by in the flash of a smile and you have nothing to prove that the vision you thought you beheld was not another mirage.

Those with faces are either dark-skinned tribeswomen or Jews, like the wondrously plump woman, always in the same brown skirt and green lisle sweater, whose ponderous crossing of the street each morning was obviously a neighborhood spectacle. In all directions, men lined the curb and, as she crossed slowly, deliberately, barely able to lift a foot, a hush would descend and with it a kind of awe, as when one sees a swan walking.

With their defined brows, large eyes, and glossy hair, Persian children are beautiful. They dart about, smile, look serious, and charm as a butterfly charms. If they are girls, their presence becomes especially important: their faces are the clues to an otherwise invisible world.

On a bus between Yazd and Kerman we came upon one of indeterminate age with a high child's voice and the manner of a woman long admired. Her props, besides her little girl's printed frock and leggings, were a pair of tiny gold earrings and a mop of henna-tinged hair. To the men she was at once child, sister, and prospective mistress. They tussled with her and held her on their laps while they teased her and fed her morsels of chicken, all to the mixed discomfort and pleasure of her equally beautiful but subdued and veiled mother. Forty years earlier a sultan, seeing such a prize, would have clapped her into his harem and left her there to ripen.

STREET EXCHANGES

Like women, public life is easy to misjudge. First, there are many venues where a nonbeliever is not welcome. Should you somehow get in, you have to hurry for fear the inevitable crowd will collect. If an impression sticks, it can seem as arbitrary as one of those illuminated pages in a museum case (chosen how?), shining up from under glass.

It is hard to remain objective when everyone insists on treating you as so much mobile revenue. No sooner has a taxi deposited you than the resident mendicants cluster around, capering about and twitching on remnant limbs. Sufficiently inspired, one of them may even compose a little ditty about you, chanted in a delicious falsetto to general merriment. The traveler who aspires to see anything must stand and hold auditions, now and then rewarding with a coin one of the more promising, who takes it without a smile, a bow even, as no more than his due, to be subjected to cool scrutiny and, if below expectations, returned on the spot.

One can't help but perceive an intricacy of social interaction as abstract and untranslatable as Persian poetry, that onionskin of endlessly overlapping allusions and sound association. The simplest transaction, such as buying some flowers or having your shoes shined, can take on a complexity that makes a Western dentist, with all his drills and sprays, look like a piker. How could buying a dozen carnations be a big deal? But it becomes one when the vendor insists on bringing out his entire stock. For a quarter of an hour the two of you pore through them until twelve mutually satisfactory stalks have been selected. Then each must be wrapped: first, in a fern leaf, next in a strip of costly newspaper. The bundle is tied together (you are offered your choice of ribbon and colored paper). Last of all you pay, a ceremony in itself that requires his going into the street to make change. Then you bless one another and leave. Pare all this away and one may find nothing—the void of the basic desert existence. Yet the carnations, your friends agree, are beautiful.

The efficacy of a street ritual dwells in a complex succession of steps. Consider the forty-minute operation of having a pair of shoes shined. The cobbler removes them, carefully setting aside the laces. Next, after placing newspaper under each, he begins scraping with what looks like a paring knife. Then, the first of three coats of wax must be applied, but not before the cobbler, like a baseball pitcher repairing to the rosin bag, sears the wax to be applied in a little brazier. Suddenly in the midst of it all, he realizes he has forgotten something essential. Leaving you, he goes into his back room. You hear him fumbling around. Finally he emerges holding a cigarette which he offers with a grace and thoughtfulness only the truly poor seem able to muster.

A WORKOUT

A man prepares himself for a life of mutual respect by working out at a *zurkhana*. It is in a back street, a one-room building containing a bench for spectators and a sunken pit where men dressed in red plaid loincloths (hitched in the middle and billowing over the buttocks in a series of folds) assemble in the evening to work out. Presiding from a raised platform is the owner, a big man in blue tights and white T-shirt. While they limber up, he urges them on with two hand drums, all the while interpolating sayings of the Prophet's son, Ali, and chanting verses from the national epic, Ferdowsi's *Shahnameh*. (Imagine Americans working out to Walt Whitman!)

After the exercises, each sees what he can do twirling a javelin. Holding it at arm's length, he begins to rotate, spinning faster and faster to the accelerating drums until the circles start to come apart and someone steps in to catch him before he falls. While the next twirls, you see him at the edge of the ring, hopping along on one foot to clear his head.

The javelin twirling leads to the final feat of throwing a great club the size of a man's leg. The performer prepares by juggling three of them. Then, when he has gained enough control, he must try to throw a single club end over end in such a way that, without moving, he catches it behind his back. Few succeed, but perhaps that's not what counts. What matters is that he has thrown it and not been brained, that he has enlarged his fund of courage.

A BATH

Another center of male life is the *hammam*, or Turkish bath. Here as elsewhere, a bath is about getting yourself clean. Still, you can be so congenitally unclean that nothing can be done for you. After being turned down by three different bathhouses—

it is Friday, after all—you find one willing to take you on. You pay, are given a ticket, and shown into a locker room whose carpeted sides are separated by a cement runway. On this "street" you must stand until you have taken off your shoes. After handing them to the attendant, you mount a carpeted platform, where he will gird you in one of those red plaid loincloths. Taking care not to step on the runway, you are led into a modern shower and left there with a bar of soap, hot water, and the door locked. The shower is not so much for getting clean—something no one can do alone, unaided—as for getting you used to the tactility of water, rare presence that it is.

Feeling a trifle disappointed after ten minutes of shower, you find yourself wandering into a room that looks like a big fish tank. The walls are a scummy algae green, the red cement floor features a squad of cockroaches methodically plodding about, and overhead, a remote glass dome lights the room. At the bottom of everything, you assume a praying position, arms tucked behind, head tilted forward, and the attendant, armed with what looks like a Brillo pad, works his way down. Each time he turns you around, your loincloth must be readjusted so he doesn't make contact with your private parts. The rinsing off is taken care of by two shaved-haired kids carrying half tires of steaming water that they hurl toward you, jai alai style.

Once your dirt has been scraped away, a coating of soap is applied. Then, after a second blasting from the tire kids, comes a shampoo. Your attendant inserts a soapstone into the bottom of a plastic bag. By dint of much rubbing and blowing a certain quantity of suds collects and is applied. But there is no actual cleaning of the scalp. Instead the attendant makes a series of smacks with the flat of his hand, as if beating a rug. When he finishes, you are led back to the locker room, while taking care not to step on the forbidden runway—else the whole bath must be repeated. But never have you felt more clean.

A DERVISH CONVOCATION

Everyone has heard about dervishes, those men of the begging bowl and silver ax. People credit them with an array of magical powers: the ability to walk on water or swallow a sword, or carry their own severed head in their arms like Dante's Bertrans de Born.

Their strongholds are the Kurdish towns of the West. In Sanandaj I am invited to witness a dervish convocation. The meeting hall consists of a plain white-painted room decorated with Sufi calligraphy and an interior room for the séance. As I step inside I am handed, by way of welcome, a large mug of tea. While I cradle it, the head dervish, a portly figure dressed in white flowing robes, holds forth on the mystical order's rigorous requirements, which he sees as a refinement of Islamic practice. After praying five times a day, they can all convene here to extend their ecstatic skills.

From the inner room come the first liquid moans of "Allah." I find a place among spectators lining one wall. The rest of the room is occupied by turbanless dervishes, long-haired faces nodding to the beat of a pizza-shaped drum. After a series of preliminary incantations, they rise in a back-and-forth plunging two-step that accelerates as extra drums join in. With each step forward, hair whips across face and chest. As in voodoo, it is the clash of different patterns, accelerating drum rhythms, dancing, and cracking of hair, that brings on possession. But unlike Haiti, where each undergoes possession on her or his own (and with definite reluctance), here everybody undergoes it together, linking hands to form a ring, in blind fraternity possessed.

At this point the head dervish steps forward, holding two ends of live crackling electrical wire. He gives them to the lead chanter, who, in a show of acceptance, plants the two live ends in his teeth. As he dances, thus charged, every now and then he makes a whimpering moan. When he has finished, the head dervish hands him a pair of light sockets. The dancer inserts his two thumbs and *wow!* the house fuse is blown and we are all, celebrants and spectators, plunged into darkness. But the head dervish has candles brought, and before long the house lights are back on and we see the same dancer, with his two inserted thumbs, proudly gyrating.

Next to step up are a trio of Saint Sebastians. Skewers are inserted through the cheeks, between cheek and gullet, and across the rib cage. After each skewer is pulled out, the resulting hole is pinched shut to prevent scarring. The skewers, I am told, are to be followed by the severed-head trick. But the possibility of its being performed on a shaven-headed youth is more than I can bear and I leave, realizing once again what little appetite for grotesquerie I have. All the same, it is hard not to admire those who, by pure discipline, have made themselves into Allah's lightning rods.

THE MOSQUE

In the Shiite version of Islam that is observed in Persia, such self-mortification is far from uncommon. But the center of religious and civic life remains the mosque—the desert reincarnated within walls of tile. Severely abstract, with inner domes composed of strands of interlocking brickwork, it has a delicacy that makes Istanbul's pencil-and-ink mosques look like railroad stations.

The central courtyard, the celebrated *eyvan,* is a bare gleaming void, a desert where for once there is water, maybe no more than a trough for the hands, but enough to give the promise of holiness. At the ends, like a distant enchantment, stand wall panels of blue tile, mirages hardly different from those of the Persian sky. As one approaches, forms emerge: large floral scrolls threaded with white; a labyrinth of blues starred here and there with a bit of orange or green or scarlet that may suggest the paradise of the afterlife. Dominating it all in a great blaze of tile is the dome. As the rays of the sun strike, the dome visually expands to become a vast circling river in which all earthly life seems summoned up and contained.

What keeps the design from disintegrating under its own luxuriance (as in much Indian art) is the respect Muslims have for the unity of creation. Thus pride of place goes not to the swelling volume of the dome, but to the narrow band of gilt Kufic lettering circling it that proclaims it part of a natural order conceived in the imagination of a unique Creator.

TRAVEL

Persian society, like most traditional societies, does not encourage traveling. Why put yourself at risk? Before embarking on a trip, the ordinary man consults everybody: his family members, his copy of Hāfez, the various mullahs and mendicants. All invariably counsel prudence and prayers.

What holds for the poor can hold also for the more privileged, only now it's not risk they fear so much as contamination. The man so unfortunate as to be obliged to travel should go by himself, in his own car if possible. When dining out, he should request a private room. To step into a common taxi is to mix. Several such taxis and you are, he believes, hopelessly compromised. You are not a man of taste any longer, but common.

The streets, to be sure, are full of those who don't mind being common. You see them squatting on their heels in the bazaar, listening to a storyteller, or in fervent attendance at a soccer match or a belly-dance performance. But a man of taste would no more join them than he would join the line outside a public lavatory.

With such beliefs it stands to reason that my friend, this man who has undertaken to show me his country, will do everything in his power to make sure that travel, with its inherent promiscuity, does not turn me into another clown. So, after a brisk tour of his city's latest hamburger stands, swimming pools, and refrigerators (rarely functional, but big, prominently situated, and glowing with family photographs), he whisks me into his new imported Impala and sets off for the rainy north and the Caspian Sea beaches, where his fellow elite sit with the look of shipwrecked Shakespearean actors.

My friend so succeeds that, after three weeks of relentless motoring, I wonder what, if anything, has struck me: a tiny girl waving from under a tree as she holds an even smaller brother; two shepherds in double-breasted suits (I remember one absentmindedly fanning a favored ewe and then, clearly exhausted, hunkering down beside her); tribeswomen in turquoise sweaters and tights, glimpsed in a rice field among huts of conical thatch; perhaps a few others in pink pantaloons, or scarlet dresses, skirts fluffed out by layers of multicolored petticoats, bouncing a melon on a hand or tickling each other.

Only once, something special: a spring-fed lake reached after a drive that had our Impala up to its hubcaps fording two little rivers. The lake was a depthless milky blue and warm only on the surface (not where the swimmer's hand stroked). But the cold did not keep several youths from plunging like kingfishers out of the boughs of an ancient sycamore. Now and then, from high in the branches, one would burst into a verse of quavering classical song, its Persian all the more telling in a Turkoman throat.

Our breakup came in Hamadan, on the way to a favorite monument of his, tastefully isolated at the end of a mountain road. As we rounded a bend, I made out the sound of a drum and then, piercingly loud over it, a dissonant pipe. It looked like a Kurdish encampment. I caught a glimpse of a circle of women in tribal dress dancing before white tents. When I asked him to stop, he retorted with a nasal "Why?" and instead of braking let the car roll on. That was too much for me and with a brutal "What else in God's name am I here for?" I leapt out.

After my outburst, I was prepared to find my own way down the mountain and back to our hotel. But when I returned several hours later, wonderfully sated by the bangled, eyes-closed, women's dancing I had watched (not to mention the series of improvised stick or combat dances that had two old women, and even a policeman, intervening to break them up), I found him maniacally polishing his beloved hubcaps. He had stayed, he said, because he wanted to spare me the ignominy of a jolting ride back in a three-wheeler taxi. It was clear, however, that my irrepressible pursuit of ethnic rituals had landed me in the ranks of common clowns. For that, he would never forgive me.

FROM ISFAHAN TO KERMAN

There are certain days when the turquoise sky of Isfahan turns an ominous white. Those days the airplane does not depart. If we ask when it will, we get the phrase we have learned to recognize: "Come back tomorrow and we'll see." For travelers who have run out of hotels willing to put up with them and their intestinal demands, this won't do. When our fellow ticket holders (a plump, personable doctor from Shiraz on his way with his mother and his beautiful wife of three weeks to Kerman "to make my fortune") propose to hire a car, we assent, glad of the opportunity to see a five-hundred-mile chunk of typical countryside.

So much for theory. The first couple of hours we found little to catch the eye other than a few pigeon towers and the occasional white-robed dervish silently imploring alms by a cross-road. Perhaps every thirty miles, a chimerical village announced itself through a screen of fruit trees: pink, white, and pale green blossoms peeping out like an astonishing sherbet. Once in a while we caught sight of an irrigation system, bunches of hat-shaped air vents making a giant's drunken path across a plateau the color of eggplant.

Five miles out of Isfahan, the macadam ended. From then on, the road was only a gravel track, or hard-packed sand with a still-visible tire mark that we clung to like a piece of skywriting. Lunar boulders jutted out enough for the road to take an occasional serpentine swerve. The rim of eroded mountains escorting us as we climbed made me feel we were traveling on a former sea bottom. There was silence everywhere. Then I realized that the car's ignition wasn't on, even though the speedometer registered sixty miles per hour—on a climbing road! A mighty wind had transformed our luggage piled high on the rack into a sail.

We stopped at a roadside teahouse in Nāīn for lunch: a thick greasy soup eaten with flaps of bread; new curds; a chicken no bigger than a hand, tough, but full of taste. We ate with our hands, squatting in facing rows on carpets from which sleepers had just been evicted. From the way everyone stuffed them-selves I realized it would be a while before we ate again.

Back in the car, turned south, I finally understood the nature of the dust storm that had been driving us. On the right I could make out dust devils gathering into corkscrews. Once high enough, they swirled away in acre-sized bounds across an all but invisible land.

From time to time wraiths emerged from the swirl: a man leading a string of camels; villagers in white face masks, plod-ding on some inconceivable errand. Of more concern was the hole in our radiator. Whenever we spied a pool of water the driver would hop out, pail in hand, while the dust roared and he wiped his hair and cursed. At gas stations the curious collected: wild-eyed urchins; listless dogs with chewed ears; even a man with an advanced case of Parkinson's, who shook while we reached into our pockets and took up a collection.

Nearing Yazd, flat roofs gave way to long-shafted wind towers that cooled off the houses. Instead of caps, the men sported turbans.

With night, the wind abated. Dust lay in blue ripples across the road, which, now and then, took a yawnlike swerve. Our chauffeur, his long torso outlined in the blue of his denims, hugged the more visible left of the road, where there was less chance of catching a wheel in a dust drift. To keep him from nodding off, we plied him with box after box of matches. He would take one, light it, and throw it away.

Around midnight we pulled up at a roadhouse in Rafsanjan, the Hotel Asia. It seemed wise, with Kerman several hours to the south, to eat something, since the wind was in full cry once again.

While the doctor and his wife argued about going on, the driver took his meal out to the car. When we emerged from our dinner, he was stretched sound asleep across the front seat. That settled it. We men would sleep in one room, the women in the other. The floor was an inch deep in dust. When everyone seemed asleep, my wife saw the doctor's mother get up, proceed to a corner, and urinate. Then stepping gingerly like Lady Macbeth, she returned to her cot.

Next morning in the continuing dust storm we arrived in Kerman and the inevitable Hotel Sahara. Completed a mere six months earlier, the Sahara was already falling apart. In our room half the plaster had vanished and the floor was awash in dust. Spanning the room was a thin metal rod of the kind you might hang a necktie on. It was, we were told, all that kept the domed ceiling from collapsing. But the garden, with its nasturtium-ornamented pool, must have persuaded investors. A bare stone terrace gave onto a colonnade of alternating pine trees and long-tipped cypresses that whistled in the soft wind.

No one before us apparently had ever come to Kerman for pleasure. We kept being asked if we were going on. To our looks of incredulity came back names like Bam, Zahedan, Karachi, all served by a fortnightly bus. Perhaps this was what had attracted us to Kerman, that it was there at the back of beyond and that it manufactured carpets: ugly, luxuriously piled ones intended for American department stores; and for the nouveau riche of Tehran, ones consisting of a repeated single teardrop.

In Kerman very little had survived the two Afghan wars. Almost apocryphal was Aghā Mohammad—the founder of the Qajar dynasty and a eunuch—who levied on its people a tax of ten thousand eyes. He had them laid out in piles and then counted them himself. The oldest of the palaces housed the American Point Four Mission. To its bureaucrats it was obvious enough why we had come—to spy on them—but for which agency? The province reminded them of their native Indiana. But we couldn't get them to tell us which they preferred.

MAHAN

That there were towns beyond Kerman we realized after breakfast next morning, when the bellhop muttered something about Mahan. Bewitched by the magical name, we followed him into the room of an enormous German-speaking lawyer from Tehran, Aladdin Sultanzadeh. In honor of a holiday, he and his clients from the forestry office had hired a car to go out to the garden city of Mahan. Did we want to come along?

Somehow or other we crammed in, four and five to a seat, perching on each other's laps, knees, even in that neglected space between the driver's left knee and the door. And off we went over forty miles of unpaved roads to reach a garden containing little more than an anonymous wall, an L-shaped outhouse, and in the middle, a little apricot tree. There, in its shade, the lot of us sat, playing games of bingo with green fruit.

After lunch and a tour of the shrine of the Sufi mystic and poet Sheikh Namatullah (with an ancient carved door, a simple whitewashed interior, and a series of cypress-ornamented octagonal pools, it managed to fulfill the promise of the Alhambra), our friends decided that the holiday would not be complete without an excursion to the fortified city of Bam, a date oasis 150 miles to the south.

Bam looked like a cross between a mud-hued Carcassonne and the set for a Douglas Fairbanks Jr. film, with narrow looping palm-lined streets flanked by twenty-foot-high cinnamon-red walls and a great gutted castle on the heights. We assembled in the room of another forestry official to be regaled with a meal of local oranges, pistachios, *loukoum,* and, of course, the famous, almost alcoholic, black dates.

We devoured far too many dates. On the drive back, we felt more and more sick with each mile. But our internal plumbing didn't finally succumb until after a meal in Aladdin's Tehran palace a week later: bourbon, chickens boiled and baked, an unctuous pilaf, nuts, watermelon, honey cakes, and the ultimate, a thick soup personally served by Aladdin and his wife.

As we listened to the thud of cars in the early morning, to the hotel servants beating rugs, we knew we would never make it to Mashhad, much less Herat, a mere 150 miles, but three changes of airplane away. Fortunately we secured the services of an old French-speaking doctor. With his medicine came a servant from the house of our friend, bearing bowls of yellow-colored broth.

The medicine and broth somehow defeated our dysentery. A couple of days later we found ourselves at the airport. We vanished into a sky where little squat towns spread like jigsaw puzzles against patches of green and barren plateaux and white amphitheatrical mountains.

When we landed in Istanbul, it was to be struck by the luxury of the city with its three great estuaries, green rolling hills, and dark heavy trees: all like something wrapped in an Asiatic veil and called woman, but which wasn't that, I knew now, but merely a mirage, or rather a dance with drums and, under the wrists, white tiny bells, the one music impossible to do without.

Dancing Outside: A Summer on Lesbos
1964

The fishing port of Mythymna, located just off Turkey near the mouth of the saline Dardanelles, could not help but prosper. Since the time of Daphnis and Chloe various conquerors had taken over, Romans, Franks, Venetians, Turks, but the good life afforded by the bountiful waters, the fertile olive groves, and pastures had always continued, marred only by the climate's increasing dryness.

Then had come the 1923 catastrophe with its vicious uprooting of a highly civilized Asian Greek culture. A political line was drawn, one with anywhere between three and twelve miles of strait in it. The Asian side was called Turkey, the island side Greece. Then you forbade all but the foolhardiest fisherman to make a crossing that for three thousand years had been every Greek's to make.

A lively trading center—the last port before Constantinople for the coast-hugging Alexandrian traffic—had become a faded, edge-of-Asia art colony village. It supported but a scant fifteen hundred souls. Its houses hugged to their chests the brittle pastel of their past and there, like an old, many-petaled rose, they sat. The villagers couldn't seem to find their knees. When with the help of a cane one did totter down to market there remained the problem of climbing back up the steep needlecomb streets. Whoever possibly could, left—for America, Germany, and, more recently, Australia. From whence money orders dribbled in, leaving a new society of pensioners with little choice but to rent out the rooms and screened-off corners of a dowry home.

———

My wife, Marcia, our two-year-old son, Felix, and I had come to Mythymna at the instigation of the Greek-American abstract expressionist painter Aristodemos Kaldis. It had been a little sketch of his, seen in a friend's home, of a pair of donkey ears peeping forth from a mound of grass blades that, long before I had gone to Greece, had given me a sense of what its country-side might look like.

I told Kaldis that my wife and I had been charmed by the Páros we had encountered over Easter, two years earlier, but we were also curious. Would he recommend another island in the same chain where Marcia might be able to paint?

Kaldis would not hear of Páros. He pointed out that the Easter landscape that had enchanted us was burnt to a crisp by mid-June. A painter, he said, needed *verdura*. As for the white streets with their vaulted-roofed houses, that may have been sculpture in Corbusier's sense, but it wasn't architecture. If it was culture we were interested in, we should try one of the few islands like Lesbos or Samos, where education was permitted under the Turks. He preferred Lesbos. With ninety-two villages, mountains and bays, and thousands of olive groves, it offered more variety.

As a base from which to explore, Kaldis recommended Mythymna, a former international art center around the peninsula from Troy on the northeast tip. It was there, he told us, that the dolphin-borne Arion had swum ashore, bringing Asiatic meters into Greek poetry. An hour's walk down the coast lay Petra, where Achilles was said to have retired in a huff after Agamemnon forced him to relinquish Briseis. In the other direction, opposite the Lydian mainland, the hamlet of Eressos clung to the cliff from which Sappho had leapt to her death. Kaldis added that in the valley below the town there was a government-sponsored class B hotel that could put us up.

I knew of Mythymna as the pastoral setting for Longus's second-century romance *Daphnis and Chloe*. But the island's proximity to Turkey drew me more than its historic associations. I had become increasingly captivated by the blueslike *rebetika* dances, which the expelled Greeks of 1923 had brought from Smyrna and which I had briefly encountered one evening in the little port of Perema, among a party of Greek sailors. On an island almost directly across from Smyrna I figured I had a chance of seeing that spontaneous dancing, "part dream, part prayer."

Easier said than done. For most of those first weeks, I feared I had come to the wrong place. Marcia was able to find a congenial life for herself and Felix at the town beach despite the raw sewage flowing out from the rampart walls. The art colony that congregated there fascinated her; she wanted to learn the relation of a man's shirt color, his walk, his whole bearing, to what he was trying to express in his paintings. For her, our jaunt had the end of discovering who she was in her new career as a painter—and as *woman,* not *wife.* But I had come for something else: not the beach, not would-be artists, and much of the time I felt I was choking with all that belonged to anywhere. I kept asking the foreign-speaking townspeople I met if the resort mentality ever gave way to a *rebetika* dance—two men, heads bent and cigarettes in mouths, at opposite ends of a huge wooden circle, weaving to a bouzouki—but they all assured me that, as far as Mythymna went, there were no such carryings-on.

I had been there for a fortnight when the mayor organized a folk dance demonstration in honor of a visiting American destroyer (sufficiently armed, its captain proudly told me, to exterminate the whole eastern Mediterranean). The musicians and dancers had to be imported from the mountain village of Aghiassos in midisland, a half day's journey away. An indication of how bankrupt Mythymna was, if one didn't happen to see the locals afterward dancing among the pulled-down bleachers. For them, the music, the smells of the grilling skewers of souvlakia, conferred sufficient festivity to make them want to dance to their own hand-clapped rhythms.

As for what it indicated, who knows. Of all Lesbos's villages, Mythymna was one of the few that did not offer a *panegyri,* or saint's day festival. And the one *panegyri* I had taken in, at Kalloni on midsummer day, seemed more like a church fair with expensive beer, horse races, circle dances, and couples dancing demure tangos. The Anatolian *amane,* or passion, I was looking for was not in evidence.

For those first weeks I was in no shape to worry about *amane.* The heat and the blinding reflections prevented any walking, except into town or down to the beach to stare sullenly into the scummy gray-green water. Even the blue of the early morning sky did not bring any escape. There were always rainless clouds about, closing off the distances in an Asiatic pall.

Now and then I'd catch the early morning bus to the island capital, Mytilini, four hours of vomiting passengers and bays so agonizingly blue my eyes smarted as if they were on fire. The glare was frighteningly present. For five hours, between noon and five, everything shut down. Not even a telephone rang. Only a dazed rooster tottered somewhere. A pale yellow stubble disfigured everything. Instead of the electric clarity of Attica and Páros, the bus moved through an opaque torpor of alkaline wastes set off here and there by a deserted olive grove or a stand of pines.

———

One evening, after we had been there a month, Kaldis turned up at our hotel, dressed in a shaggy shepherd sweater and twelve-foot-long crimson scarf knitted, as he announced, "by the thousand virgins." Over dinner he gave our surroundings the once-over before querying in his gruff fashion, "How can you, a poet, be living a mile out of town in this pseudo hotel? You'll never get to see the real Lesbos here. You should be staying in town." For a moment I was speechless. Wasn't it he who had recommended our hotel? But what he was saying so corresponded to my feelings I could not risk getting him off on a tangent. Instead I asked, "How can we stay in town? There are no hotels."

"Why stay in a hotel? All you need is to rent a couple of rooms in someone's house." And he proceeded to tell us about the pasha's palace where he and his sloe-eyed Nota were staying: deliciously cool, two-story-high rooms with painted ceilings and shuttered views looking out toward Turkish Troy; the prettiest garden in town, with almond trees and serpent mosaic floor; not to mention an orchard with a flock of sheep and goats. "The miscreant who owns it," he went on, "is a retired police force colonel. He is said to have collaborated with the Germans. He and his wife, the ex-pasha's daughter, help support themselves by renting out rooms."

"Are there any available?" I asked.

"Across the second-floor hall from us there's a pair of rooms that should suit you and your family. Why don't you come over tomorrow afternoon around five? I'll give Marcia a painting lesson and you can write a famous poem about it."

The next afternoon, on his garden balcony, I found this pot-bellied bear of a man huffing about in his bathing trunks. "Where have you been all this while? Making love?" The sally delivered, he turned, slapping his belly for emphasis. "Look at this splendid physique. No one would say I was sixty-three." The accusations, as it turned out, were a smokescreen to disguise Kaldis's own unpreparedness, his lack of even a brush. But then, as he said, he hadn't come to paint, but to write his memoirs.

Our watching Kaldis over his shoulder as he painted on a

canvas he had tacked to a cardboard box reminded him of how in the midthirties he had watched Matisse in his Nice studio, the color values changing with each applied stroke like a game of rapid, end-to-end soccer. Only for this Greek, the painting was less a contest than a spool he unraveled, gingerly, strand by colored strand, out of the Platonic sky of his conception.

Taking a dab of red on his thumb he implanted the kiss of a poppy field next to some martial olive. A few more strokes, a pair of kneelike rocks, and, at the bottom, a bay's oversized starfish. There remained only to look at it upside down and on its side as he placed it in the balcony's half shadow, then against the full cream of his bedroom wall, seeking which of three possible categories it would fall into: "work of art," "masterpiece," or "miracle." Followed, calmly, by "five hundred dollars" and a title that would grow ever more mysterious: *Sappho's Dream, Polychromatic Wood.*

Next day we moved to the Colonel's. For all the convenience of its situation and the beauty of the grounds, the palace had its drawbacks, not the least being its owner, whose pink-faced portraits in sword and full-length military regalia hung all over our second-floor hall. Retirement from the police force clearly hung heavy on him. When he wasn't sitting on the porch in his baby-blue pajamas, he was likely to be turning off our taps or provoking blood-curdling screams from the twelve-year-old servant girl, his shepherd's daughter. As a result of domestic economy (conserving bread by turning it into delicious pastry), his wife had grown rather massive and, as he said plaintively in his high-pitched French, "Who can make love to a bulldozer?"

As I accompanied Kaldis about, up one or another street picked more for its chance of shadow than any directness, I learned his story. Born in Turkish Dikeli, he had moved to Lesbos at the age of nine, remaining until sixteen, when he ran away to join an uncle in Alexandria who was in the cotton-shipping business. After three years spent mostly at sea, he had come to New York, settling in Hell's Kitchen. It was a difficult area to prosper in, sleeping in shifts in a flophouse while educating himself in public libraries. How he got into union work I don't know, but during the depression he helped Diego Rivera organize hotel workers. Rivera, in turn, encouraged him to paint—small canvases the size of a forearm. That left the rest of his considerable person free to concentrate on his self-publicity, that bohemian figure to be encountered any evening at the Cedar Bar or by the door among the coats and red-and-winter-purpled faces of a gallery opening.

On the lecture circuit, Kaldis was wont to talk about the "restless serenity of the artist in his studio." In his own person, "serene restlessness" seemed more apt, as he was unable to sit in a café without bellowing at some passing nymph, "Beauty, come sit down!" When Beauty, to her own surprise, found herself drawing up a seat—age, after all, has its privileges--he might add in his best artist's manner, "You have lovely eyes and thighs," with outstretched paw rubbing the latter as if they just might be blue or green. Followed by a further flash of paw, "Those panties, how much you pay for them?"

Beauty isn't a New Yorker, she won't say. Undeterred, Kaldis feels them. "Not silk are they? Why not? Silk too expensive for you?"

"Yes, I work for a living."

Fatal mistake with Kaldis to reveal the vocal chords. In a jiffy he pounces. "Oh, so you're not an artist, are you? You've got no man to support you. Your daddy's not rich?"

"Oh, yes, he's rich. But he doesn't want to support me."

"So you're an heiress," Kaldis rejoins, hands punning insolently among the long tresses. "What does your daddy do, own supermarkets?"

Bit by bit he would drag out the whole spoiled, sheltered

story, seeing whether he could enroll her in that not-so-exclusive sorority, the Daughters of Kaldis. To him a woman was a castle, awaiting assault. And it was that prospect that got the blood once more coursing through his piratical organ.

With Kaldis about to explain history, or how a poplar grew (by jetting a bubble toward the sun and leaning on it), I began to appreciate where I was. I even put aside any thoughts about seeing the *rebetika* dancing for which I had come. What concerned me was writing about the round of a day: how the countryside got up, dressed itself, and went about its several tasks; how morning spread, a gold soft mountain ring within which I stood, a pack of cards in hand, writing.

———

Awakening. Time, so new, waits. Child-yellow fields glow. The first rose, they say, is about to be born. After that—a green hen? Walking along the port I watch the night's little fishing boats dance into their stone pockets of shore. Farther along, a villa's white-tubed, pink-roofed outline swims all by itself.

Over the cups of shadowed hillside, mountain peaks rise, pencil sharp, a skating line of pauses and sudden, ash-pointed leaps before collapsing on a sea clean as silk.

There, at the edge of vision, three headlands float. Each of their shadows forms on the water a great leaf which, as the sun strikes, visually reverberates like a gong.

———

Out of a café's beaded curtains men advance, plastic *komboloi* beads tucked within slim behind-the-back-held fingers.

They hold their lies stretched in each other's pockets. They make roosters vanish with their calls.

Sunfry shirts. Orange suspenders. A donkey draws up and the owner jumps on, to ride down a dung-yellow street and out where no breakers rumble. Just stubble, a peasant landscape's small butterblue houses, waiting. For the flask of a shirt to come and tie the goat to a pail, the farmhouse to the lid of the morning.

In town, shop gratings are clanking open. The grocer is green aproned. His voice holds all his shelves contain and tosses it.

Up, where brooms splash in the silver of a courtyard. Tree and ladder down. To me, standing below the ramparts, colored by an hour that softly, for the wind in the almond branches, sings. Like hay and I, a child once again, seated high over a stubble luminous as that peasant threshing far below with his one, his four round-circling horses. As I watch I feel my hands turning into a butter, grown that golden. And the midmorning over which they turn is one where each thing stands in its tall cone. I swim. You, Marcia, on the beach draw up your knees and wave.

The old man has his baggy knickers on, his whiskers curled. Around his middle the yellow sunsplash of a cummerbund. Later it will turban his head as he turns in the slow yoke of the threshing.

I see him as the essence of roundness. Well where he sits in round keglike boots while, gloppity-glop toward him, comes the true master of things, donkey. His sovereign stands there dominant, rush hampers gleaming like a large moustache.

The late morning strikes and rolls toward me a white. Bell. Carried on its bubble of sound I walk down through the town gate and out where noon rages like a turkey in the long wicker grass. There, if shadow still lives, it is as spade, as sparrow. As those field women's stooped black basket shapes.

Secrecies of the siesta: wine and flies.

In the shadowed courtyards silence flicks a broom, backward, forward. Blinks. Raises its head, its donkey eye. Passes a bright grape of light through its mouth and, satisfied, lies there, chest calm, feet color of smoke, and hair, the very happy hair, still.

When your family weighs on you too much, you can always go somewhere else. One charm of a Byzantine culture is that, wherever you go, a café, a barbershop, it will be human sized. Shape of a hat with a pencil-slim body pulls up before an awning with its jacketed, crab-scurrying waiters. Or inside, where walls are a photograph-festooned pale blue: royalty; heroic whiskers. And on the marble tabletop, a glass of water. Water and card slap. Farther off, reflections: shirts, wool suits, elaborate whiskers, astrakhan hats. Waiting in their frayed togs for something. The next earthquake.

"I like you, come sit with me." Like the idiot, the stranger you are, you accept. He is the pilot, you the shoal. No, he is a jewel case you hold. His name is George, fifty-sheep-he-owns-them-George. He is nuts about *rebetika* and dances hypnotically as you know, having one evening surprised him and his cousin, Strato, in the fishermen's café, cigarettes in hand, circling to a *zembeikiko*. One of these days, he says, he will rent you his mare and you will go off together to a *panegyri*, that spot of music in island somnolence.

And away he goes to tend to his sheep, and a nap turns on its slow sun-spilt hands.

When I rouse myself, there is still sunlight flickering through a porch's morning glories, chickens ambling about, and on the stoop sitting nearby, two old and walnut-bright faces.

The liquidity rides. Soft blue against the letters of the trees. White and gold where my invited, jam-and-fork-eating self sits, trying to imagine what it must feel like to be so many feet from a dowry's end: red, budlike nail in the hourglass dusk sewing.

Start. And stop. Let the needle in. And count. And make something small and bent like a fruit tree where a goat's hooves climb. Then in the quickening day-end walk, thinking of friends who have already emigrated where a girl does not have to wait for spring and a veil of white blossoms to offer herself.

Turn, reassemble, and now with your friends, three abreast, parade among the churn of red, nickel-screaming bicycles. Or pause and talk to a kid whose legs bend from a wall. Count on the mouth of the wind horses—a manes-and-tails-stretched, olive-shaking grove. Then let brightness shine, brightness that is more than the olive trees' blue, tossed, sea-cantering shapes; more even than a bay with chaff like so much icon gilt upon it; so bright that only in moonlight can it truly glimmer and become *tsiftetelli*—two sailors, arms twirling over the head, fast legged, dancing it. Dreaming of whatever the dolphin in them dreams—a Mytilini tart with breasts that tinkle bells and a huge guitar of an ass.

When the day has finished screaming, when the last goat and fence have retired, time (old man who wears his white trousers low) comes, takes off his things of salt, and writes.

In your socks not far from him, you sleep. The world and the beast in you have separated. Only sadness is, like a calm, quiet dessert.

Take it in your hand now and go.

By early August I had come upon a number of shepherds who were, like George, *zembeikiko* fanatics, willing to talk about it, and, when the spirit moved them, to dance. They weren't able to teach me because that dreamlike zigzag striking requires *kefi,* something that must well from within. (This is why few Athenians know how to dance it.) But now and then in their company I would totter forth from a table, improvising out of what I had observed. The strongly accented rhythms provided a containing circle within which I could look over my shoulder and copy, or answer back. But I had no way of dancing for myself, nor any inclination.

Mid-August, time when *panegyris* are bursting forth almost daily from the pent woodwork of a summer. For the Feast of the Virgin, George and I have resolved to go to Aghiassos, as its folk troupe would indicate that people there can dance.

Unfortunately, Marcia and I had arranged to give our own end-of-summer thank-everybody party on the eve of the feast. There are a violin and accordion played by the village barber and his brother, her friends' Beatles records, my local friends, her bearded artist admirers. Discordant elements. For most of the night we hover on the verge of a brawl. But my musicians weather the insults, and I don't get home until 4 A.M. When I wake, some hours later, the bus I counted on has long since left.

Undeterred, I tell Marcia I'm going anyway. Walking on my cork-soled beach shoes if I must. And I point in the direction of Aghiassos and the two ranges I must cross.

"But you're drunk and in no condition to go anywhere. Why don't you stay here and go with all of us tomorrow to the *panegyri* at Petra?"

I reply that Aghiassos is the island's prettiest village and a *panegyri* there should be worth attending.

"How long will you be away?"

"Maybe two days—if the first is good."

"All I can say is that you'd better be at Petra, or I won't answer for the consequences."

With throbbing head and nothing but a notebook and a bathing suit in a satchel I head down into the little dell where last night's expensive café looms. Over a needed coffee I ask about my cashmere sweater, flung aside in the midst of a dance. Not there, but the girl obligingly points to another, same general green, new on a hook. Proudly, forgetting the mountainside where I am headed, I turn it down and stamp off down the sweltering road toward Petra.

With each mile I grow more apprehensive: of the sun overhead and the decreasing likelihood of hailing a car or a motorcycle big enough to carry me over the switchbacks to Kalloni and the chance of a taxi. I am on the other side of Petra and starting to climb when I opt for a shortcut along a forest riverbed.

A dancelike exhilaration fills me, of the joy that I feel moving, jumping, in woodland shadow, through pale pointed color. Where the breath is the one that licks to itself the stone over which I, a slow fish, swim.

Emerging at last, I see the road ahead of me mounting in a series of black heat-reflecting coils. Dreading it and the walk down on the other side in the treeless glare, I decide on another shortcut: along the hill crests to the midisland market town of Aghiou Pareskevi, a town closer to Aghiassos, and one I have never been to.

What about losing my way? Well, as the crow elsewhere flies, so must here the donkey trot. When in doubt as to two paths I have only to go where droppings lie thickest.

Before me nothing. Olives. Nothing. Olives. Occasionally

cobbles. White and Roman looking and going nowhere. Or a high, equally white, broken-neck bridge. But no houses—nothing that still has a roof. And no people other than a surly peasant feeding a bag of small pears to his horse. And, hours later, the silver bell of a herdboy, asleep in his shirt under an olive tree.

Stones, hills, sunlight, olives, strung like so many beads out over the blue. Throwing spoons of shadow into the air and catching them. Pretending it is still First Time, well where I sit, the ring on the finger of the day, the smile in the ward, the white oven of its silence.

As I pick up my journey I am conscious once again of the sun blazing over this one, hoof-white, donkey-dung stone gulley of a path. I feel the sun burning in my throat, calling me into the fields that I have entered for their softness under my feet, the fences before which I must stop, lifting one leg, now the other, as one might a suitcase. I burn, I fidget with the bathing suit I've tied like a moth around my head, and on I come, the pathway below crookedly wavering like the whitest of sheep. That stupid, that much to be followed.

Finally in an hour that is just the dung shapes of horses asleep in a distance that glitters mice and hay-shaved stubble, I find it, a Quarter-Mile-off-the-Road Farmhouse. Into its squatting, tobacco-separating family I burst, demanding in my best wolf tones, "Water." Which comes after a moment's hesitation— seven pure, silently filled glasses. Then a melon, its white cap removed, and presented with a spoon. When I have gouged out the last green ounce, what can the family do but whisper something to the girl who has fetched me the glasses? Fearing it, the unrepayable generosity of the truly poor, I get up and, with a smile of thanks, trundle off.

After an hour's walk along a glittering white track I reach

Aghiou Pareskevi. At this hour its blue-shuttered streets are empty save for two young men, arms around each other's shoulders, quietly, shyly bicycling. Further on, encountering a lady, I ask if she knows of a restaurant that might be open. Not only does she escort me all the way across town to the main square, but, to my astonishment, goes behind the counter to dole me out a small icebox's supply of tomatoes and feta, and the water for which I must keep humbly asking.

A nap now? I am directed to an adjoining hotel. After being shown the five beds, I pick the one with the longest sheet: so soft, each time I adjust a cloud of dust puffs up, while a parade of flies struts in and out of my nostrils and along the pursed banks of my lips.

The country under me, half asleep, is the magical one paintings inhabit. Where I am me, light. Light and roses, those about my horses' upturned trotting necks on the way to that great shrine, *panegyri*. Which beckons, open and bright. Open with peasants, with carts, with icons and cakes and toys and shops. Bright with all the light an orchestra, or three, or five, can pour into it. If the sky is falling, then call its fragments the pieces of my luck. Held outstretched before me like a glass and pitcher, a plate with its white cheese and black olives.

Should a waiter hand me a wet clear spoon I would not look up. What is around me like clay, like olive trunk and shadow, is more than enough. So I watch as the others, forms too of light, of new clothes and hair, stroll. Stopping to talk to a neighbor, they stand, waiting for late afternoon, when the music will begin.

As they circulate in that water-weave among stalls and trees that is any *panegyri*, I begin to understand why I am holding a table. For what a *panegyri* gives in the course of a day's dancing may be nothing less than what Marx and Engels mean by the "withering away of the state." Only what in Engels is utopian jargon is here a reality.

Not that such a dissolution happens right off. The landscape, the ongoing four-thousand-year fact, must be established. For this, tradition decrees a horse race. Imagine a road dense with people, several even in the trees (by a field post, crouched on the flat of his hands, a photographer). Now in pairs, quick as a telegraph, flash Percherons ridden bareback, Parthenon-frieze style.

With the first darkness comes more crowdedness, more tern-flash of waiters carrying round platters of shoe-leather beef and expensive beer. And the orchestras begin, at first playing arranged medleys, then, with the coming of evening, dance tunes addressed to the individual paying dancers.

The floor now? Moonspit, white, strawless. Forms bow, spring, make their moonflicks and are gone, whence you can't say. In all of this there is intelligence: weaving movements; ironic match-flame fingers. Then, late, it may happen, the abolition of a landscape which is a peasant, alone on the great white of the floor, dancing his *zembeikiko*.

What will have impelled him onto the floor is hard to say. There will have been the long night, the music and its alcohol. Slowly, he has felt something welling. With a half gallon of wine in his throat, fueled by the kerosene of the orchestras and the whole worked straw-churning summer, he gets up, pockets his matches, and, with cigarette in mouth and his two women by him (the wife in a dumpy brown dress, the daughter in a sprightly red check), dances a folk dance. Ceremonially almost, for the benefit of the surrounding tables and every dead person within stamping range. Then, this ritual observed, he lowers his head and stands, while all around the people, wife, daughter, friends few or none, fade away like dreams, like the parched rubble of stones, hens, and who knows what of his daily life.

He is there, standing. The music above him, a great black

cross. As he starts to dance, he takes something from his hand, wipes it once across his trousers, looks at it. Then with foot he says something that crashes on the floor like the word *spit*. When the floor doesn't answer back, he takes his best palm and with it. HITS. Down across his life, across all that the books and others say he is: shoes, floor, black of nail, trousers. Hits, smashes. And the floor, like a wet green log, like all his face and trousers, flames. Flames and becomes the sizzle of an ouzo glass someone offers him. Together in the moonfloor silence he and the glass's giver—his wife—drink. What he has been doing is setting fire to himself. And not only to himself, but to a landscape of which he is the shadow made flesh. Made hair and bones and forty-eight years of age and now, grasshopper-style, dancing. Creating spoon, fork, apple with a red center. Creating with every gesture something new, not of this world, and now by him, for the eyes of all within drinking distance, spun, twisted, erected. I am me, he says. I burn the knife. I cry.

———

After three-quarters of an hour in bed, I stumble out past a grinning hotelkeeper. In the square I come upon some youths, hair properly combed and a sweater folded over the shoulders. On August 14 that can only mean one place.

"Aghiassos," I ask, going up to them, "how are you getting there?"

Small cups of smile as understanding hits. A maroon-colored bus lying under an acacia is pointed out. Am I to understand that it will take us there later in the afternoon?

At 4:30 P.M. magical letters, AGHIASSOS, go up, and to a burst of songs from the boys in the rear the bus leaves. The road under the olives like a ladle turning, dipping. Past fat, smacking, zlack! cigar-dust Kalloni plain. Where the color darts, stops, as the embroidering needle spins, and over fields makes. Swallows.

Makes a glistening tobacco and horse-dotted plain through which the road winds, up over dale and down past. Hoes. Peasants by them, peering from soft petal-brim hats at an afternoon, just their brick-colored shirts, their threescore oranges. Pop them against your throat, feel them bursting.

And donkeys. Long ones with dark skinny tails and spots and where-to-pin-it signs. Who look up expectantly before lapsing into containing shrubbery.

The road, a dance rhythm, bends, dips back on itself, turns. Transparency is in its gown of fat bell-thick olives. Blue shadow goats here. A stork, black-on-white apron-wing, upfluttering there. Or a road worker, a red flower in his teeth, hand on hip insolently standing.

At an old oak tree crammed full of canes, umbrellas, girdles, and bras dear to Saint Anthony, we turn up toward the Olympus range. As we swing past people with tents picnicking and a series of rose-festooned, uphill-trotting horse carts, I am aware of a distinct sylvan presence. At the bottom of Aghiassos, in a beech-shaded square full of pilgrim buses, we emerge to taste the mountain sweetness.

The walk up the cobbled street is steep enough for eyes to explore: fruit stands boasting hanging nets of big green "American" apples; candy stalks; local pottery; a bobbing visual feast that all the same does not prepare me for the jam-packed crush of the cathedral yard. I expect to be searched at the walled gateway. Instead there are girls selling white crosses. Along the rim of the cathedral, pilgrims are already sprawled, elbow to elbow, sleeping.

A steamy, pushing line conveys me into the great clanging cathedral interior. On the marble floor families are picnicking on grilled chickens and chewing watermelons. Around them a wonderful mob circulates: vendors of holy items; children tingling bells; bearded, miter-hatted priests in pink robes abstract as stars.

Seeing a candle-holding line part company for the chanting priests, I decide to join it. Finally I am by the glass-encased Icon of the Miraculous Virgin. I plant my candle, stoop, and kiss the sacred glass, to be rewarded with a sprig of basil, while a second lady squirts my spot with disinfectant.

With the basil tucked behind my ear, I head into night-fallen streets. In a large mall near the bottom of the town three orchestras are operating over a floor never wider than ten round feet, where one virtuoso couple after another dances and waiters, trays in hand, cross.

To me the dancing seems contrived: white-shoed types up from the big city to do a rehearsed number; then, since floor space is at a premium, shift to the next café, where the same display of dips, turns, leaps will be enacted. Dancing more because their image demands it than because for months they have been thinking of little else and it's now or wait for another year. For me, meanwhile, there is the pleasure of circulating, sitting wherever I can find a chair, and exchanging English conversation for homemade bread and stuffed eggplant.

At 3 A.M., on my shivering way to the corner of piled rugs I've rented, I run into two guests from the previous evening's party. Their good cheer kindles enough to relaunch me. Uphill first, to check out a hilltop café. Then back to the mall. We arrive in time to witness a peasant *syrtos*. Two old knickered men are dancing, or rather jumping, in what looks like a shower of ouzo, while to one side a young blade in city clothes stands clapping, flamenco-style.

For twenty minutes, tirelessly, as if dunking for apples, the two go on. When they are through a young man with a bit of sailor in him (among his table of blades I have noticed his pawing feet) stands up and executes a magical *zembeikiko*. He follows it with a fast, finger-snapping *tsiftetelli* belly dance that has the surrounding twenty-five of us gasping, faces lit with shy smiles.

In full daylight to a stampede of splendid single dancers the orchestra goes on playing. At seven o'clock they manage to control themselves enough to call it a night. Even then there are men still needing to dance whom for another half hour I watch, turning en masse before a jukebox. At that hour, as we all know, anything works.

———————

Hard to leave Aghiassos. Especially when noon reveals more isolated dancers turning outside a shop, a café's slanted cobbles. If a few are like this now, what will the town be like by evening? I feel torn, wanting to see what a sustained festival will offer, whereas at Petra there will be dancers I feel closer to, having shared their landscape.

To ponder it I go order some cakes in a pastry shop—battle the yellow jacket. He wants to kill himself, I want my breakfast, let's see who wins. Fifteen minutes later it's the yellow jacket and I am headed down a blue-balconied street to the bus depot.

How to tell which bus goes my way? Does it matter, since they all go down the mountain and once at the oak tree I should be able to hail a ride? With a policeman's help I find one willing to deposit me there. Only the junction comes, goes, and we are several turns beyond it before the driver realizes that the freak indignantly rapping at his window panes is me.

On my tattered soles the road is a heat-reflecting bowl here and there enlivened by some festively dressed peasants, or a gypsy couple, the man leading a small larvalike child slumped over a horse. Finally I'm back at the junction. On the wrong, but shaded, side of the Petra road are two ancient seat-white stones. Perched on one is a tall, moustached man, a shoulder-folded coat demonstrating that he, too, was at the *panegyri*. I ask how long he has been waiting. An hour, the man replies, irritably. About every ten minutes a possible lift pops into view, only to veer off toward Aghiassos. This doesn't bother me; I need the rest and enjoy sitting on the stone, wiggling my feet in the afternoon light. Sooner or later, I'm convinced, a car headed our way will come, and we'll flag it down.

The chance to test my theory comes sooner than I expect—a jeep appears, headed uphill. Which fork will it take? I hunch forward, ready to spring into the road. But I haven't actually moved, and when the jeep turns up the mountain, my companion, who has stood up, lets out with an enraged, pavement-rending stamp. Then he walks over and says something like, "When a car comes, any car, get your body out in front, understand?"

Do I? Less the actual words than the rage such a stamp, abstracted from the dance floor, inevitably conveys. Up to that moment, I had cultivated a passive transparency. I was a mere vessel for the words that might rain down on me. Others appeared complete in themselves, but I, a writer in process, was not. Suffice to say, I had no idea what gave a man his gumption, the courage to go for it, *do it!* Now I understood that a man, in any other man's eyes, must be his strength. We are not all equally capable. But we can each use the strength we possess to smash into so many fragments the nonexistent, because-I-say-so irreality that surrounds us. The smash of a foot, of a hand, may be mere signs of frustration. But, rendered absolutely, they can thrust open a door.

We were both on our feet when, down the road from Aghiassos, came the very Aghiou Pareskevi bus of the previous afternoon. With the same handshakes and grins and reddened faces, deep in new purchases, aching limbs, and winey yawns. Through the olive groves for an hour we rode to be let off where the road separated, five miles from Kalloni.

In lavender light, my new friend and I walk, lit by the far cube of a white farm. My companion tells me that, should I be so unlucky as to miss the bus, he will give me dinner at his home and then whisk me on his motorcycle over the mountain to the *panegyri* at Petra.

Farther along, he stops to light a meditative cigarette. Finally a question, innocent enough: "Do you like grapes, figs?"

Seeing no harm, I admit as much. Next thing I know he is plunging across the field. Three red dripping bunches of grapes have been cut when, wanting to help, I proffer my satchel. For an instant he hesitates, then with an air of absolute finality surrenders them to my satchel. But it is not until much later, clambered onto the special bus, I realize what I have inadvertently run off with.

The grapes are juicy, they run. Next day, when I take my notebook out of the satchel, a whole summer's jottings have washed away.

Petra is jam-packed. Unable to snag so much as a box to sit on in the music-drenched beach cafés, I join the *volta,* where the same baby carriages, the same male and female hopes, whirl again and again into view. The *volta* has a rhythm that eludes me, caught up as I have been in another kind of walking. But a *volta* is no more about walking than a siesta is about taking a nap. The idea apparently is to move your feet slowly, as if musing, now turning to talk to someone, now stopping by a well to take a puff, while all around the dream life stirs: round-faced girls with black-beaded eyes and costumes perhaps only possible as thought out in the secret fastness of a dresser mirror, who stand expressionlessly conversing. Groups of walkers turn, reassemble, and now, arms linked, walk, rearranging themselves into more and more solid collections of white shirts matched to black hair, trousers, shoes. Walk, meet people, smile, what those minutes on any sidewalk after a church service are: seaside civility.

Still, a *panegyri* is more than its *volta.* As I stand noting possibilities—each orchestra with its own long movie theater of packed tables, its distantly flashing dancers—I wonder how I am ever going to get close enough to see anything. Then I spot tables migrating through the packed throngs, firefly-style. Not long before my head, pleased, is bearing one, legs in the air. I plunk it down under the nose of the shrilling clarinet, where finger-blast whistles flash, most with somersaulting trousers, shirts, empty beer bottles, wan giddy smiles.

The evening starts making sense. Retsina is called for. Nervously, it might appear from my perspective; surprisingly and wonderfully to the table of half-drunk shepherds beside me. In the next moment a watermelon appears on their table. Hardly cut, divvied up, and here is a photographer, here are we all arranged in a great horseshoe of lifted glasses: cigarette, pearl-like, in mouth and head up, as in heroic, nineteenth-century *palikari* poses.

When the last bulb has exploded, let the drunkest of the lot, short, with hose-thin shoulders and perfect straight teeth, ask me to take the floor with him (he has run out of partners). I agree on condition that I be allowed to drink the three half-liters I need. I'm finishing the second when my friend, who has a bus to catch, stands up. Our first dance is a languid, walk-behind-and-gawk *politiko syrtos,* a dance to get me used to the floor, that it is there, that I can be calm. In tribute, I suppose, to my foreignness I receive an exaggerated amount of ouzo, the dancing each time mercifully stopping as some shepherd stands up to proffer a glass. When it's over, my friend calls for his own wild, clarinet-filled *tsamiko.* It is the dance of his friendship, of all that he will do for you: pitch from your handkerchief; crawl between your knees, head tilted up star-wise and cigarette still squarely in mouth; followed, maybe, by a somersault from full standing position with only a kitelike handkerchief to hold him up. Not feeling up to such trust I ask one of his friends to replace me and sit down, knowing I must still make the long uphill-tottering walk home to Mythymna.

———

The summer is a great net I have pulled around me. In its last recesses I sit. With reddened eyes I hold the sun. An orange goat ties me to his tree. When in ten days my flight leaves I should be ready.

As it turned out I still had a way to go before I could stop the momentum I had set in motion. I might feel I needed to slow myself down and recover my sanity. But in the *panegyri* season being mad is nothing. A whole segment of society is, and they were not about to take my "no" as final.

Three days after the *panegyri* in Petra an Armenian guitar-playing couple arrived in Mythymna on what must have been their yearly visit. They had hardly begun to play in the bottom-most of the rampart cafés when I found a shaven-headed *mikri* come to rouse me at an unlikely four in the afternoon. "Music," he said, "you must come, George sent me."

With little choice, I followed the lad down to the café. There in the midst of a bunch of weather-reddened shepherds and fishermen I found the whole George family, holding an empty seat, as if specially reserved. Some twenty feet away, the Armenian sang Smyrna-style *amanes* in a deep, belly-wobbling voice. It was what I had given up any hope of ever encounter-ing and here it was, a voice from the legendary past conjuring laments over which one or another adept glided, bent, dipped.

For three blissful nights the Armenians played. When they left, I knew I had experienced something of that lost Smyrna of Seferis:

> We anchored by shores steeped in nocturnal perfumes
> Among the singing of birds, waters that left on the hand
> The memory of a great good fortune.
> —"Argonautica," translated by Rex Warner

A day later, as I dragged myself, soaked with sunlight and sea wind, up the steps of the pension, I was met by a distraught George. His striking eleven-year-old daughter, Eleni, whom we had engaged to baby-sit for our two-year-old son, had been sexually attacked by the Colonel. What the attack consisted of—an attempt to kiss her? a mild pawing?—was unclear. But her convulsive sobbing had brought George, knife all but gleaming in its duty-bound scabbard, to our room. He regretted letting Eleni work for us. The Colonel was, after all, notorious. "As it is, there is not much I can do. I'm a poor man." I was in no mood to lose our baby-sitter and I promised him I would do what I could.

The Colonel was nowhere in sight when I went out. But early next morning I found his baby-blue-pajama-clad self pleasantly sitting in his garden chaise longue.

"What do you mean," I said, speaking French, "by attacking that eleven-year-old girl?"

The Colonel laughed benignly. "It was nothing, nothing. Don't worry about it."

"Nothing?" I asked in the most mute of whispers. Then, after a moment's staring at the stone floor, I spat. Pointing to the chaise longue to show that he was that spit, with a single stamp I ground my heel into it. As the Colonel recoiled, cringing, I added, "If you ever touch Eleni again, I'll personally strangle you." With that, I turned and walked upstairs to my room.

That this braggadocio succeeded had much to do with Kaldis. Was there ever a canvas to which a few flourishes couldn't be added? Miffed that he had not been on hand to take it in himself, he consoled himself by going down to tell the Colonel what an athlete he had sleeping under his roof. Whether this included a Golden Gloves pedigree I'm not sure, but it was enough to extract a payment to George for his wounded dignity, which allowed Eleni to return as my son's playmate.

A day later, by way of thanks, George asked if I would like to rent his pregnant mare and ride over to Magdalena for a *panegyri* in honor of the saint who year in, year out, for that one tall August 24, shines. Saint Fun's Day. Saint Drink 'Em Up's Day. Saint Black Vest and No Tie and the hair like George, a whole Gray and Glistening Pomaded Olive Tree.

Let our goal be three headlands in the haze, dimly, lionly, stretching. Mark on the longest of their forepaws a town. Call this the Nipples of the Magdalena and you will be as accurate as stone houses and pink-tiled roofs and lots of peasants sitting on rush stools under grape leaves can get you. Then again, a town known for its Watertown, Massachusetts, gangsters can be rather defiant, as I already knew, having ridden with Marcia through its rail-high, café-crammed alleys and trembled for my very stirrups.

It is midmorning when we arrive. I have dismounted to drink from the fountain at the town entrance when, from a café, there comes some Australian: "What, my friend, are you doing here?"

I reply, "I'm here for the *panegyri,*"

"You're out of luck, man. There ain't no *panegyri* today. The *panegyri* was last night. Many people, cars from as far away as Mytilini. But today there is nothing."

He invites us to sit down and sip lemonade.

I find myself fending off the usual curiosity. How rich am I? How come I ride over here—not for the *panegyri* certainly! He laughs his Australian laugh and talks about his hotel business back in Sydney, about everything but the *panegyri,* which I see steadily disappearing, down the street, into the drugstore sun. Before it can disappear utterly, I am on my feet, almost rudely parted.

Halfway into town the strap holding my saddlebag gives way. I am on my knees gathering my effects when I become aware of music from back of the barn and the 3000 B.C. sunrise, in dissonant brass exploding. Leaving everything (all day various odds and ends will be returned by anxious-eyed townsfolk) I head off toward what turns out to be a café's seven-piece unelectrified orchestra: trombone, parade drum, accordion, bouzouki, guitar, violin, and over them, making the grape noise that hangs fat and purple on all the streets, clarinet. That long, that high in the sky, pointed.

With the band are twenty middle-aged men in white shirts and vests and horse-heavy shoulders. The face bluish, upturned at the nose, and, if you want, Balkan looking. With a mountain in it, that cliffside to which Magdalena's shoebox cafés cling.

Into this, without a by-your-leave, I enter and in the obscurest corner root myself, saying, "Retsina, a half kilo, please, and some tomatoes." With the food come the attentions of a pair of urchins who don't know what to make of a man sitting all by himself, who poke me through the blue window with straws. But before all the evidence is in, the waiter has shooed them away. This leaves me in my corner, unmindful even of George (who will come in grousing, "How did you expect me to find you?" and, even more obliviously, "Why here?"), growing more and more my two hunched elbows, my refilled smile; wider as the dancing goes on, continuous poem and I'm writing it. On my shoes that want to, but don't know how.

It is past noon when the café, led by its owner, a great cloud of a man in white shirt and suspender-held gray trousers, finds itself seized by the need for beauty; utter beauty, picture-album beauty, the whole party spilling out into the street in a handkerchief-linked file. Before a bemused assembly of canes and black-suited, whiskered, three-day-red faces they dance a *kalamatiano*. Among them the café waiter holds out a tray of tiny, opaque-white glasses. And for the rarity of the day they quaff. Then on in weaving rings they spin, leaving only George and me and the band in the café.

Next cancel the town awnings with siesta: orchestra and dancers dissolved and the cobbles now just a lot of canerush stools filled with little men with black torn vests and shepherd crooks and plenty of sheep breath under their wool socks, plenty of red faces. Let George pick out as friend the reddest of the lot, who offers to find us *kreas,* "meat." When three butcher shops have somehow proved insufficient, he invites us to his own place in the bottom part of town.

Here in an unadorned cement yard, among circling flies, we sit, while the two women of the house remove our shoes and hand us, as gestures of welcome, sprigs of basil to be sniffed like a perfect martini. Soon even meat appears: a turkey, led on a string. Nods of approval and minutes later the turkey reappears, still on two feet, but headless.

While the turkey is being dressed, the noon demands. Its own white sausages. Supply them and, while you're at it, lift up to the grape-trellised roof a table, chairs, plates, and ouzo bottles. Have me in my clumsiness break something precious like a plate. "*Den peiraxi,*" I say, wanting to put them at ease. What does matter—the bowl of beans the daughter graciously serves? Oil is dripped in, the father pouring: a bit, no, the whole grinning can. There on the roof, by piled firewood, the three of us eat, while overhead grapes melt into the red tile of the surrounding roofs.

Tiredness is a sail we hold by a cord at the end of our fingers. Through a tiny dollbox window we climb, to stretch out on a floor's length of cloth and embroidered pillows.

Waking a while later, I slip out through the window and into the street. I'm walking along the promontory above the cafés, gazing at the olive-necklaced hills of my earlier walk to Aghiou Pareskevi, when I hear the notes of a *serviko,* wild and grape and digit-fast. I follow it up a snail-curl of streets to a ladder-reached trellised roof, where are gathered the men and band of the morning café. Who greet me with, "This is my Cloud Shoe father's roof, what can I do for you?" said in an Australian accent that, among these white-sleeved, moustached presences, doesn't seem quite so offensive. I point to the orchestra that has gathered round and say, "I like music—that fast Balkan *serviko* they were just playing."

"Oh," he says, brightening, "you dance then?"

"No, I just like music very much."

Unable to believe that a writer can be his two quaffing eyes, he persists, "But you must dance something—a twist, with me?"

Driven to the wall, I reply, "Twist, no, a *zembeikiko,* maybe."

Whereupon a tall stork of a man in old-fashioned ripply white sleeves and black vest asks if I will dance one with him. Quickly, in a tense silence, I down three glasses of ouzo, and the musicians strike up. My performance is what one might expect, a little too breathless, too full of disjointed slaps and leaps which leave me rather red faced when, minutes later, the musicians decide to call it an afternoon.

We file down the ladder behind them into the street where we reassemble parade-style, five abreast. Turning into a little street, we stop before a green house with an iron railing. While the musicians serenade, Cloud Shoes's wife comes out, bearing a silver tray adorned with glasses of ouzo she will offer to each of us in turn. Since there are not quite enough glasses, you only touch mouth lightly to the rim, then reset it where the next can taste its opal brilliance. And the procession moves on, winding from one family doorway to another, before each of which messages must be poured into glasses, set afloat in our thirsty hearts.

For dinner, we repair to Cloud Shoes's café, sitting outside on a ramp above the evening strollers. A lamb fresh from the spit is brought and choice morsels are placed in my mouth—fingers, forks, smiles.

We have reached the watermelon course when the Australian, who has been translating for me, asks if I will draft a "dying mother" letter to his consulate, requesting a year's visa extension. Surprised by the turn of events—this morning nothing would have seemed less likely—I go with him to a corner table. When we return, I am one of the family. I'm even offered a room for the night—but what about George?

The crowning accolade comes from Cloud Shoes, inviting me to dance a *zembeikiko*. From a man whose dancing had so impressed me, that's unrefusable. The bouzouki player looks up, nods, and at that moment my initiation begins. Try as I may, I cannot not dance. His great cloud of a belly holds me, gives a target toward which I can direct the angles of my head, shoulders, feet, bringing them just as close as I can. A raft of glasses pours down, but fearing to lose concentration, I postpone them until the piece ends.

What else do I dance? The intimacy suggests to him a *tsiftetelli*:

> Cross your legs and think of what you'll do
> Eat your mother's whiskers beat it in the blue

Lightness, a line of customers amusing themselves outside a brothel on Saturday night? Gaiety my head shakes with, my fingers whisper, as this woman's music plays, coiling me into its fine shadow-lace, its mounting, heaving clay.

I am there, a rose in sunset standing, when Cloud Shoes asks what else do I dance? Silence, I can't think of anything. But it would be impossible to go now, the floor would be so cold. As I hesitate, the orchestra strikes up the very *serviko* that had brought me to their roof hours earlier. While Cloud Shoes stands to one side, clapping time, I, who have seen this two-step danced only once, do it by imagining my feet hobbled together like a horse. I hop until the sheer speed of the music has turned the blades of my feet into a pair of skates.

When I stop, unable to breathe, there comes an immense crescendo of offered glasses. Looking through so much ouzo is like looking through smoke. Breathing it is like breathing mist. The last quaffed I return. To our table. To what the night still has in other cafés to hold out: I wriggling on the floor, knees forward, neck thrust back, while over me Stork Clothes or George or the Local Idiot dances with an elegance, a power, I help make happen. When the policeman silences the orchestra at 3:30 A.M., I go on dancing with a young kid to a rhythm provided by two tables of women's and children's clapping hands.

The green field stabs me to a smile. The orange womb looks up, higher. It may be dawn or the end of the world, but I am falling asleep.

Sleeves and music. Sleeves and music battering in my skull.

———————

Waking, huge. Feeling quick sun, shadows. Drunkenly penetrated by white oblong shirts, smiles.

I put on my own shirt, went down a flight and sat. Back in the café, a yellow herbal liquid. Served in a tall glass with Melba toast and taking an hour to empty.

Outside, I discovered that the streets had during the night mysteriously fallen down. They lay on their backs, disheveled, grinning, and occasionally a bit of blue or purple spit flowing off a near wall illuminated them. I took in the effects cautiously: toe, next toe, moving on points down an embankment that yesterday had seemed street, a *kalamatiano*'s sizzle of dark and spinning figures tracing deliberate dials over pocked and glasslike stone.

I sat down in Cloud Shoes's café and ordered an egg. Stared at it awhile and upped the order to tomatoes. A full plate! Then walked, or rather curled my feet back to the previous café. Where there was my tea and everything was white square stone tables and mermaid and record singer calendars and pale, fairy-tale blue walls.

Silence swam through the café and created something ship-like, but hulled in air; as much a part of the cliffside expanse as of the tin mugs and small-windowed doors. Swam and changed the figures who came in, a bouzouki in muted, siesta-observant hands, to relationships of space and glass. Their space, my glass. And the BLACK in and on that space means STAMP touching you crowbeards, dream turning far below in the urn soft silence.

Turning, touching, as in a wave of the hand, a good-bye, one into the other. Parapet wall along which once again I am walk-ing, past two faces mounted on brush-loaded donkeys, arms waving toward last night's dancer a hearty recognition, "*Pane-gyri,* today still, why are you leaving?"

Down over stubble fields I walk, greeted by the green foun-tain of a poplar, the blue gourd of a peasant shirt. Happiness, I think, is not the Simplon Express, not even with a glorious, hip-wagging Barbara Stanwyck in it. It is something with strokes, hours, the perfect, because perforated, grass of song. Tall stick and I'm holding it. In my liquid hands, my gigantic moon-colored eyes.

———————

A last afternoon comes. I have intended to spend it walking in the Daphnis and Chloe valley below the town. But as I march past the last café I hear an unmistakable hiss. Deep in a sprawl of glasses are four moustached faces. One lifts his ouzo and says, "Magdalena, I saw you dance, sit down!" while a second points to the black music case by the wall, indicating he is the town's bouzouki player, in eclipse since the evening shortly after arriv-ing when I saw George and his cousin briefly dance.

For one last afternoon we sit. The table is plain donkey gray. The chairs are rush. In them they are, as sunlight is.

The waiter brings ouzo, whites of cheese, plates, shirts. We catch it in our held, smiling, tugboat-banged glasses. "*As pethanei o thanatos*" ("May death die!"), clinking toasts until the floor seems so many shards, the waiter not exactly smiling as he crouches, sweeping.

Around us a music develops, slow and enduring and calm; calm as trousers, as eyes, slits in a room where nothing is except coffee, except glass, except the reaching, exchanging slap-slap of card on table.

All very promising for the start of a final evening, were there not George come to remind me of the farewell feast his family has prepared for us.

Off we reel to George's home, where, among the morning glories and the priceless twilit view, I find Marcia. Fretting and letting me know that, no matter how many the courses, she intends to be out by 9:30 P.M. to say her own farewells. Not, I would say, reckoning with a peasant feast. When a family tenders you one, you are meant never to rise from it. If you do, there are always the gifts, the embroidered tablecloths and pillows, which you must answer as best you can with cosmetics and nylon stockings and shaky promises to send more once back home. A feast isn't a feast, it's a lynching. Unable to do it cleanly by rope and throat, they do the next best thing— make sure that when at 10:30 I do leave for the café, it is with my hands hooked around George's and Strato's helping shoulders. There by me they sit (making sure no other family can get through) and next morning they are all at the Colonel's with smiles, waves of the hand, and baskets when the taxi arrives to take us away.

We are a few miles down the road when, looking down, I notice how black my hands are. From last night's dancing, Marcia explains, the much-smacked, sticky floor. With this memory rises another: a man in a ten-foot circle of chairs and weathered faces spinning, his hands white drunken plates in a sea of viscous blues, reds. I realize that in the course of the summer, I had touched, broken through to something—a world unlike anything I could have expected. It was up to me now to create out of those much-touched, shattered floors a danced mosaic of my own.

Zambia: Bars and Barflies
1971

The travel itself by Land Rover through Northern and Luapula Provinces I could well have dispensed with. Bush is bush and on roads where any hundred yards was the same as the next hundred miles there was very little to look at. On the top of a dangerous, endlessly straight, gun-barrel road we drove, rarely meeting anything but an overturned truck or a pair of mallards quacking up from a pothole.

People were likewise few: four million in a land that, by some estimates, could hold fifty. In the villages, young men had gone away to work and we encountered only women and children and the old. Since the soil was poor and farming was of the semi-nomadic slash-and-burn variety, there were no permanent houses. For centuries, the people, a few warrior tribes aside, had been cattle, traded from place to place as slaves. Unlike West Africans, they did not seem to have systematic beliefs that related sexuality to nature. The medicine man was someone you consulted only when all else had failed. Belief centered in the tribe, its hierarchies too fragile for the new Coca-Cola cash economy.

Fortunately I had a pair of binoculars. While my friend, Tony Oberschall, interviewed small-village businessmen for a sociological study, I was free to wander about, using birds, butterflies, garden flowers, and the people's own clothing as a start toward putting together a local palette. Of course a traveler can find color anywhere. But in the streets of Italy or Iran it may seem more a matter of buildings and park railings and local fashion. It does not emanate, as it did in Zambia, from the forest pool of the skin.

Among women I saw beauty as a creation of curved features modestly receding under tall conical hats and water-star earrings; pond-shadowed eyes; the nose, a blunted mountain, softly luminous; turbaned hair, pin-curled in rows like the streets of a thatched village. Against their black stillness a piece of jewelry resonated, vibrant as the snap of a twig, as a thrush calling.

My four-year relationship with a much younger woman had just ended. In contrast to its sexual aridity, a new Matisse-like world of sex without strings beckoned: bodies, mango smelling, thin as a slice of water, a series of drops on polished stone. Or an orange shirt that, in accentuating a palm, made the muted rose-black of her forearm glisten.

This may not be the place to defend the pleasures of anonymous sex. But just as bird-watching requires binoculars, so before bodies so dark, so shadow hungry, one has to get up close enough to run a hand over erotically placed circumcision scars or reflect on the earrings, tiny red globes a prostitute entrusts to you with a smile. Exoticism, when mutual, can be a license to discover sensations pressing in where all swims and rains and dissolves.

To find prostitutes, I had to frequent the bars they ornamented. In Zambia, bars have become the national institution. No one we spoke to had ever heard of one going under—and new ones kept popping up with names like Don't Be Jealous, Stretch Your Legs, Save Your Neck, and the one that says it all, Come to the City of Kitunsha Bar; names that may, or may not, suggest the varied attractions of gym-sized, cement-floored, furnitureless rooms in which the one distinguishing feature might be a raised corner platform set off with mirrors where men or women separately performed.

A much-feared violence comes from the bowling-pin-sized bottles of beer. Beer is the one drink a bar serves and comes only in that size, or even larger Congo-smuggled bottles. Recently I read that President Kaunda, the founder of Zambia, threatened to resign rather than preside over a nation of drunkards. But if you ask a Zambian why he goes to a bar, he will probably answer, "To joke." Much of this horseplay is traditional; so, if a member of the Leopard clan reaches into your Rat trousers and gooses you by way of greeting, nothing need be amiss. It's his prerogative and you will have others. But in the new towns such gestures may give rise to a scuffle.

Fighting is so common that often proprietors have two adjoining saloons: one for fighting and the other more polite, with female company: high-school girls on vacation, divorced tribal princesses, mothers wearing diaperless babies like health certificates on their backs. These waitresses, or bar girls, are called prostitutes. The term means that they don't belong to anyone and aren't local. I never knew one not to accept what I had laid out. Our interpreter, however, had his own rules: never pay under any circumstances, and never say when you were leaving town.

With such casualness, and no common language, there could be misunderstandings. I remember one tense walk under a full moon back to my hotel during which the girl and I were followed by two men who had been waiting for her to finish work. The men, one of whom was a cousin, the other a fishmonger, kept insulting her. When that failed to get a rise, they tried to shoulder us off the road and into the ditch. Meanwhile, she kept whispering reassurances: "Don't be afraid," the one phrase she seemed to possess, before launching into "One Zambia, One Nation."

But her plea for interracial unity was clearly falling on deaf ears. As we turned up a long hill her pace got much brisker. We were near the top when she bolted in the direction of a building lit by a single bulb, which turned out to be the local police station. We men cadged matches and gave our ages and occupations— to our giggle of disbelief the fishmonger, a young-looking man, gave his age as forty—while the girl, speaking quietly in that African way, explained she was being hassled. Finally, after some forty-five minutes, we set off on a path to my hotel with the policeman leading the way. While the men conferred on the porch, the girl once again bolted, to lock herself in my room.

To weather such harassment can make for a bond. But the emotional advantages don't always compensate for the beer you have drunk while outwaiting everyone else, which turns lovemaking into the progress of a salmon gasping his way up over waterfalls. Not that the girl hasn't been well coached. And for sheer willingness in reviving a limp penis she has few rivals. She raises her knees until they are up over your shoulders. She makes her labia press out like an elephant trunk. Before you know it, you are sucked in, not knowing by what right all this is being done but willing enough to accept the hardening miracle.

But a percussive sex, with shoulder-propped legs and the vagina compressed to its drumlike minimum, can make you feel as if you are being stretched out on a railroad track· bang, puff, smoke, steam. There until morning's fire lights the skies you contend, trying to score as many leaping hits off her back wall's bull's-eye as the beer allows.

Yet sex needn't be so rushed. With any stranger, there is a distrust, a foreignness, that needs to be overcome. So you may pass time sitting on a park bench, her legs enveloping you, until the warmth of trust, the mutual exoticism, can begin welling up. To put you at ease she may start asking questions: "Are you married?" "Do you have children?" Not to be outdone, you ask her about hers (all prostitutes have them). There can be other experiences you share. Neither of you is exactly a native here.

So the two of you converse in the most limited English, she

perhaps showing you some of the scars of her trade—bite marks, a broken incisor—until she feels free enough to lean back, offering you her breasts. It is the final assurance she needs, and it will carry her through a warren of mud passageways, not to your room, but hers. A gay pecking on a pane by way of a knock, a rattling of chains and you are in with sister and baby, you a large foreign dope standing in the corridor, knowing by whose invitation you are there, but feeling little sexual arousal in your beer-depressed body.

To give your penis time, step out into the courtyard's lake of mud, knowing that the whole sullying sequence of splashes must ring in tenement ears like the rudest of phone awakenings.

Meanwhile, arrangements proceed. Places for spectators have been found. Theatrically, a red curtain material is floated across the head of the bed, leaving a passageway to one side. She has already peeled off her nightclub clothes and is in a white slip: what she wears, she explains, for those whom her large body might offend—those like you! It is also a sign of what remains withheld, like those surprisingly sweet kisses with which she now and then favors you.

While I play with her stockings, she starts grilling me. The one thing she requires in a man, she announces, is someone who won't evade. (But if I didn't want to evade, would I be here, in this country, gloomily facing the sheets? Isn't my humor based on a certain sneakiness, a dance into not exactly meaning?) I am pondering this when she asks, "Why didn't you dance at the club, don't you like to?"

A bit miffed, I answer, "I like some dances very much, but rock isn't me."

"What do you dance then? Show me!" For a confounded instant in the little passageway I comply, miming a *zembeikiko*. Unable to continue under their scrutiny, I slump down on the bed, feeling this beats most anything in precoital rigamarole.

Appeased, she tells me her opinion—"A *gege* man"—and calling, asks her sister for confirmation. So the two inspect me sitting on the edge of the bed in my shorts.

"What is *gege?*" I ask. As the two dissolve in giggles, I begin to suspect it means the sort of guy who comes on as a child, sword lost in the stone.

Now that I know the worst, she turns off the light; I roll into bed, to be warmly, even passionately, received. From stone to star, in an incomprehensible well-being I rise, a kingfisher poised over water, rattling his colors.

Then sleep, heads on a shared pillow, faces turned away from each other like brothers.

After waking and leaving enough cash to mitigate my absence, I slip out (past signs I will have to remember) and down to my hotel to wash up. Next, to a café, empty except for two thin girls chatting at a table. Watching them, I realize what I should do. I buy breakfast rolls and, with a shirt and an extra wallet as presents, return to the apartment. From then on, everything is extra, the photographs they show me, the sex for which I climb back into bed while she squats in her favorite position above me. As a final treat I am offered her daughter's six year-old crotch to kiss: "A local custom," she calls it.

It is my last couple of hours in the country, but perfectly at home, for once, I sit, watching the room brighten through the sun red of the bedspread curtain and baby-sit the daughter in the mud yard, warding off her efforts to inspect the burnt stick of my penis. In the presence of these kind women, I feel more bewildered than ever. But who asks that sex, let alone sex with a stranger, make sense? I'm surrounded by gestures, I don't understand any of them, but I'm perfectly happy.

Madagascar: Life in the Red Lane
1971

There are any number of reasons why, on a trip to East Africa, one might choose to cross over to this large, red, eighteen-tribe island located some 150 miles out in the Indian Ocean. Mine went back to a dream about lorises I had in 1968, at the time of the civil rights demonstrations on the Berkeley campus.

I had first become aware of lorises, small nocturnal-feeding primates from Southeast Asia, through a friend's physical anthropology course. But the large-eyed, black-torsoed, leaping animals of my dream, I realized on waking, were not lorises, but lemurs, a prosimian unique to Madagascar. It was perhaps inevitable a punster in my dream machinery would seize on *loris*. If I found lorises beguiling, what about the Loire, the river of poets, castles, and the purest spoken French! In a jiffy I was in France, on a bank of that river. But something new, a sense perhaps of where my real human loyalties lay, managed to return the dream to those lemur-lorises and their dense, copper-leaved rain forest. They were, I knew, my ancestors, and from the verge of extinction they were crying out for recognition.

Still, I was not prepared to be greeted at Tananarive's airport by a battalion of jungle-clad, tommy-gun-waving French paratroopers. They had been called in to help put down a tribal revolt in the far southwest, a region of strange baobablike caudiciform trees. Some days later at a rally I heard a captured chieftain say the last thing his people wanted was to revolt against the island's government. But how else could a starving people call attention to their plight?

The countryside I found myself in was plateau, hill encircled and in mid-April rather chilly. Only this was wet plateau, cut into tiny pond plots, each with a farmer in it (often up to his hatted, blue-shirted neck in the mud, he and his bullock) or some twenty fully clothed women. Over a kind of raised dike the road wound, past houses of orange brick with maroon- or brown-painted balconies, tall and thin like those a child might draw.

To this Indonesian Madagascar was added the downtown exoticism of Tananarive with its hordes of stalled, honking *quatre chevaux,* its café awnings and soccer posters. On a vast traffic island, across from the restaurants and French hotels, flared the white umbrellas of the Friday market, or *zoma,* said to be the world's largest.

After leaving Zambia, I had continued to travel through East Africa: Dar es Salaam, Zanzibar, Arusha, a bus with Masai into the Serengeti. I was astonished to find myself hurtling past all cautionary lights, past unmistakable opportunities to *Stop . . . Look . . . and Listen.* Finally on the island of Lamu, off the northeast coast of Kenya, the inevitable crash occurred. That it was a dose of clap and not AIDS, as it might have been five years later, was indeed fortunate. But it made me feel all the more isolated when I arrived in Madagascar at the beginning of a national holiday with my illness still untreated.

I don't know what I did the first afternoon in Tananarive. I probably spent it slowly walking around the fringes of the market, depressed by the Asiatic misery: women who sat all day on a stairway nursing three oranges or four piles of nuts (constantly rearranging them, moving them up into a better light), or just nursing a pair of children and a begging hat. Where, in that, could I start? What would I do?

The second day, I decided to take in a soccer game between

the national team and Malawi. The roofs and staircases outside the stadium, which lay cupped like a lake at the bottom of a crater, enabled people without tickets to see the game. And the human dots in conical straw hats perched on the stone steps that led to the former queen's palace probably outnumbered the thirty thousand of us inside.

The game itself was more of a pitched battle than a game, perhaps because the substitute referee, a Malawi official, did not dare exercise control. But the storm on the field hardly took precedence over the one we made. In the course of three hours, not twenty feet from me, two men died of heart attacks. After the game, the losing Malawi team had its bus stoned. At one point the field became entirely covered in expensive oranges and the players went around, glad for a moment's respite in the heat, picking them up and punting them back into the stands.

On the third day, a Monday, I visited the hotel doctor. He confirmed gonorrhea, prescribed a drug that turned my urine purple, and forbade any alcohol, pimiento, or sex for a week. There was also a course of four daily injections.

This regime with its noon injection—two quick slaps on the butt to make me relax and in with the needle—helped me settle down. It is hard to go far when you have only half a day. Soon I began to appreciate Tananarive. Not that this was difficult; during my stay I never heard anyone speak badly of the city. For one thing, there were few police—one hundred in the whole capital. The sidewalks were not disfigured by dogs or broken glass. Downtown was, of course, a shrieking crater, but the hills offered a quick escape. And once up one staircase or another, I entered a residential serenity of arched churches and gay, maroon-balconied, orange-brick houses too steep for cars and big stores.

Prostitutes made themselves known with a friendly "*Etes-vous bien?*" or showed availability with a burst of song. The local art was raffia weaving, and there were baskets for books, for groceries, and even for the head (inverted, with a pair of strings or a ribbon tied around). The most hatted were the children, a sign of oriental vulnerability to what, by African standards, seemed a mild sun.

I came to admire the market vendors, perched on crates before little piles of bananas and bitter oranges, each arrangement so delicate it might have been a collection of marbles. Much of the rest of Tananarive had that same child-colored fascination. Orange and maroon somehow created between them, as roofs rose against the hillside, a slanted shadow within which the Merinian set himself off: black streaming hair, eyes like yellow glinting suns staring out of dark skin from a doorway.

––––––

Each afternoon, out of respect to my dream, I would take a bus out to the botanical garden, where the lemurs had their zoo. For hours, I would stand watching them, with their long erect feathery tails, as they hopped about and vaulted over one another or sat large eyed in their barbed-wire preserve, patiently grooming each other. If I had a personal coat of arms, they would be there, on a branch, leaping.

––––––

I hadn't yet spoken to a native when, on my fourth day, as I huddled between two buildings during a brief squall, I found myself accosted by an out-of-work road engineer. My telling him of the record he had broken seemed to inspire him, for he promptly invited me up to his house. He was in town to see his uncle, a radio official, about a loan so he could buy his baby a can of Similac.

There to the radio station we went, to learn that the uncle had been left cash short by a recent operation. I volunteered what was needed. Holding the can triumphantly between us, we staggered up a half-mile-long staircase to a house set in the rear of a small courtyard, with a separate kitchen that afforded a spectacular view of the whole city.

Having wormed my way into their home, I was not about to let a lack of funds stand in the way of the hospitality that in other circumstances they would have offered. If they had no food, I explained, I could buy all five of us a meal for less than it would cost me to eat alone and badly in a restaurant. These arguments carried the day. Back down the endless staircase we went to borrow a red tablecloth and purchase the needed ingredients.

Despite the hazards of cooking in a courtyard in the dark—the main meal must have been lunch—a town-colored, red-and-orange meal was produced: a salad of grated carrots sprinkled with lemon, followed by a broth of ginger-flavored vermicelli, with the remains of the broth used to cook the main dish of rice. My new friend did the cooking himself. Merinian men, he explained, are naturally domestic, giving children baths and sharing in all the housework except washing and ironing.

My host had too much pride to invite me for the second meal he had promised. But my tongue had been set loose, and next day, while poking around the vacation-closed university, I asked a student if he could recommend a hotel—a native hotel. In a way that was to seem typical, not only did he give me the name of one, but he personally escorted me there.

From the start, I enjoyed my new hotel with its Vietnamese restaurant and popular bar. My room, with its vast lopsided bed, I occupied almost stealthily. There were dressers, but I never used them, preferring to spread my belongings in a heap on the floor. What thief would want to rummage through a slag pile? Soon I was acquiring new material for it and even reading there, my goods functioning as bolsters.

Out in the street I became once again my eyes, my head on a long-necked pole peering into commercial recesses. And when suppertime finally came, it found me ready to take a place at my hotel among others. A water glass, a napkin in an empty bowl, a dark-wood crocodile ashtray, these calmed even before the bowl of hot water, with its sprig of watercress or grape leaves, arrived. And I noted the folded butterfly napkins, the design carved on the ebony grandfather clock, the grisaille-painted corner panels of moonlit houses and empty courtyards as beheld by a returning ghost.

The hotel became my passport. I had only to mention where I was staying for invitations to be offered. Astonishingly, the chance acquaintance would actually turn up a fortnight later to take me to a Sunday cock fight, or to a popular theater, a few steps from the slum dwelling where a French-educated ceramics professor whom I had met at an early morning bus stop had been born. At this theater, for the first time, I understood how a communally responsible art might work.

Imagine a large, open-roofed building with white-and-lilac walls, a few tiny paintings, and the sign "Don't spit on the walls." Most of the center is taken up by a pennant-hung stage, big enough to accommodate a troupe of fifteen actor-singers. Around it, on tiered benches, the populace sits, spitting out orange seeds as they chat. They participate fully, yelling encouragements to an accompaniment of tossed coins, shrieks, and dovelike moans.

The rear of the stage is draped in orange cloth. One of the two competing troupes is likewise robed in orange, with black-banded straw hats and flowered shawls flung over their shoulders. During the performance, musicians keep their hats on, whereas actors leave them in a circle in the middle of the floor. Directing from a scorebook is the local Verdi, an old man in a royal blue uniform bemedaled like a hotel doorway. The troupe are peasants from one of the twelve surrounding hills. And they are not ashamed to proclaim, "As you know, the rice harvest is on. If we trip up, it's because we haven't had time to practice properly."

The Madagascan is constantly telling you his shortcomings—not out of masochism, but because, like an athlete in training, he is working toward a future goal. Because everything can be put off, nothing, not even death, is final. There are none of those hysterical scenes, women throwing themselves weeping onto a coffin or jumping into a flaming pyre. In Madagascar a man dies and is buried. That's all right, we'll be seeing him later. At a time of year when the stench isn't quite so bad, his folk assemble for a final party in which they take him out of his box and, one by one, dance with him.

A shifting box of colors best describes the impression made by the deep, fifteen-person chorus. Everything is performed in unison, but there is always somebody new standing in front of you, holding up the palm of a hand, lifting an eyebrow. And singing, singing with such vigor you wonder how he manages to stay in one piece.

The material comes from the same sort of uplifting tripe that Sa'adi collected in the *Gulistan,* that is, *The Tale of the Honest Orphan.* But the unison gives the story the strength of a mass affirmation that each actor successively embodies. These performers don't hold themselves above the audience with drivel like "We're artists." No, they are just like us, all the more because of their weird, orange, nineteenth-century frock coats. What is more democratic than the past? It is the voice of the ancestors that delivers homilies with such sincerity, such bare feet and golden smiles. Made gripping by what is common, the performance distills a marvelous fraternity: we live, we are one, we can be good. Imagine fifteen voices shouting that, punctuated by huzzahs!

After I have seen both competing troupes perform, a kid I met at a bus stop a week earlier comes up to me, a fighting cock under his arm. Off we go, following a track made by small shoeless feet through the rice fields. His cock, he says, is small, but very brave, undefeated in six fights. On the way, to make conversation, I ask about the scars all down both arms.

"Made by roosters?" I ask, naively.

"No," he says, "Madagascan women."

Compared to that sort of bloodfest, a cock fight may seem rather tame. Ours takes place in an abandoned rice field, the tiny rise of the dike forming a viewing area where men squat, with children in front. Behind are women with carts of food. A compote-sized potato salad, served like a curry, its tomatoes, carrots, herbs, and greens afloat in water, may cost a penny.

The pairing off—a matter of size—takes place while the handlers gather in an oval ring. Then comes the placing of bets. The fight, punctuated by respites for dashes of water (over crest and feet), ends when a cock turns tail, something the cock is loath to do since at that moment he becomes material for the family stew. But how passionately the audience enters into it! Each rise in the air, practically each peck, elicits flamencolike shouts, exclamations, or moans of disappointment.

Rice requires intensive cultivation. You don't burn down the bush and throw out some seed and call it a day. The same intensity radiates throughout Madagascan life. Everywhere you look there are people running. The ricksha drivers, or the pair of boys with a great side of beef slung between them on a pole, you might be prepared to discount. But not the waiters hurtling, trays in hand, out of kitchens, with the look of sprinters coming out of their blocks. Garbage men lope alongside trucks, and even little girls, normally the most sedate of creatures, play between the curbs a game of grasshopper leaps and much wild scurrying which is to hopscotch what badminton is to tennis.

In some countries a bus ride into an area like the Betsileo Hills would be a matter of some trepidation. Here it is more like a festival. Eight rows of us are all crunched together like olives in a jar. Should a passenger pop up on the roadside, everyone grins and squeezes over. The steps to create a feeling of community on the bus might seem but the most halting. Perhaps a man produces a bag of peanuts from under his jacket, or a peeled orange, and silently offers it. Or to general embarrassment, an old man with a ravaged (syphilitic?) face taps me on the shoulder to ask why he can't have any children. Maybe a man in the rear starts singing. Or we run into a downpour so fierce the side flaps have to be lowered, blotting out any view. Then in the middle of nowhere, we pull up by a small river: for a piss, a stretch? No, so the women can get out, every single one of them, and, standing in water up to their waists, wash themselves and their underpants. Little things, but they all mount up, and such is the momentum that, long after you have arrived, you keep running into fellow passengers only too pleased to invite you to a bar, a movie, a stroll around the block.

Such hospitality is not confined to those with whom you have shared a bus trip. I could not go for a walk without having countrymen leap out of the bush to offer me something: a cake, a couple of hard-boiled eggs, some freshly roasted peanuts. The Madagascan can do this with intrepidity because he has no fear of being refused. One can see in this a slyness, the pleasure, perhaps, of watching you lose face. But it may also be a way of expressing trust, of saying one is not afraid.

As one goes south, the plateau of rolling hills and rice fields changes to a thin line of mountains. Houses seem to have more fantasy, more orange or red flame in them, with bits of functional design stuck onto the outside in the form of a ladder or outside staircase. Rice is still grown, but cattle now dominate, long-horned, hump-backed, black-and-white zebus. The people remain largely Asian, but with a rounder cast of face than the Malays of Tananarive. Herdsmen dress in pinks or apricots, with a half globe of a hat for the sun that seems almost to glisten with friendliness.

A row of herdsmen with long, serpentine crooks, glinting hats, and sunset-tinged robes standing against a background of poinsettia trees and cayenne-red earth made a picture of serenity that I found irresistible. The farther I journeyed, the happier the smallest incidents made me: an old man in a straw hat dribbling an orange with both feet through the refuse of a market, or a group of men with umbrellas hooked in the backs of their shirts belting down red rum in a bar. I was able to catch only a little bit of that red tonality, but I could see that people in Madagascar had achieved something rare.

A Trek in Nepal
1973

Of a holy place I ask that it give me a ground to dance on. If not with my feet, then with my eyes, plunging them into submission, charity.

To arrive for the first time in the streets of Kathmandu is bewildering. Have I ever seen such fire-and-lightning caps, a green door, a spinning wind? Colors race about, turning each street into a visual fountain.

Perhaps one has caught something of this in the riot of a spring meadow, the leaf-flash of a fall road. But in Kathmandu the phantasmagoria is people: blue people, green people, red people, orange people; more flash of canes, necklaces, caps, belts, bangled arms and ankles than in the most eye-popping Persian bazaar. Each worker is his moment, bright eyes in red-beaded calm, standing by a construction project or putting out a cigarette in a hotel lobby. To struggle about under a great bag of cement cannot be much fun. To do it while surrounded by comrades, each clearly a spoke of light, might almost atone.

But glow as Nepal's people do, they are members of one of the world's poorer societies. One can see why, in the fifties, the governing autocracy might have chosen to reverse its policy of exclusion and welcome the hard currency we tourists brought in, useful in purchasing salt, medicines, fuel, and other essentials. As observers, too, we may have had our uses. At a time when, across the border in Tibet, the world's greatest theocracy was being summarily erased, Nepal needed all the live testimony she could muster to assert that she wasn't another Shangri-La.

The catch was the pollution we brought with us. Our wants might not have seemed exorbitant: an apartment, perhaps, among the old city's knobbed and curling pagoda roofs, where tea could be served to a few friends. But the top-floor views pale before the blare of the taxis. Introduced originally to serve the airport, they have multiplied to where Kathmandu is one endless honking din. And the taxis have their needs—for oil, asphalt, a house for the driver in former rice fields. The resulting pollution makes the ring of surrounding mountains only sensed presences for months on end.

If I can't avoid the pollution, I can rise above some of it by hiring a bicycle. Suspended in a cooler air, I join a gliding, giraffelike throng that leaves me free to peer over the compound gardens while checking out the sidewalks: Thamangs in baggy, pita-bread-colored garments, set off by a black vest and lightning-flash cap; Newar women like hibiscus-hued katydids as they shuffle along in gauze transparencies, all woven mountain mist and camellia-plaited hair.

Other sights conform more to legend: the great, ear-flapping, cloud-swift stride of a tame elephant, or a lone man in the river gravel, with brush and bar of soap swabbing a prized water buffalo.

———

Better yet, a walk at dawn. First, a pink, smoky suffusion. It rapidly takes the form of a pumpkin sun shining through a cold haze where each sound hangs as if sculpted.

By the roadside women appear, rose kindled, blue gathered, stooped to their ablutions. Small, barefoot Thamangs scurry past, bent double under leaves and faggots—the second hands of destruction.

Beyond the city, rice terraces fan out in steep, curve-bladed rivulets, lime brilliance set off by a plot of mustard or potatoes. But no path or border to the houses, which seem to rise helter-skelter, flowers occurring on an upstairs ledge, pink against a bedroom's oblation bowls and religious pictures.

Farmhouses, too, are tiered in a wash of cinnamon over yellow, leaving the sharply pitched thatch roofs to make them one with the surrounding green. Even more lovely the way, above the bare threshing floor and animal-hitching posts, a pronged upper story swells, as much a vase as a house.

———

Everywhere the floating ships of temples. They are architectural songs drifting up out of the fields to the dragon-cloud sky.

There are specialized temples. For women, Buranilkantha, where a pool contains an enormous stone statue of Narayana lying on the many-headed coils of a naga. Of all the gods in the Hindu pantheon, Narayana is the most seminal. Terrestrial life is Narayana's dream, his creation. But in thin mountain air, with equatorial sun blasting down on his black body, the most creative of sleepers may get somewhat fidgety. It is the women's job to ensure that his dreams keep him asleep. All day long, a constant stream of attendants pore over him. They change his golden sweatband at noon and again at sunset; they clean him, fan him, douse him with incense and perfume, paint his feet with turmeric, his lips with vermilion; each with a little breast-sized teapot sprinkles him with anointed water or stoops to kiss his great nasturtium-wreathed feet.

For us men, there are the visual satisfactions offered by the pagodas of nearby Patan.

First, a series of terraces. They help get the petitioner used to the idea of being there, prostrate, hands pointed forward, touching, drumming, beating. Seven flights up, adrift in a cry of white flashing pennants, a gold crown awaits. The whole open-sided in-between is a tossing, totally hypnotic dance of swaying orifices, swelling plenitude. Birds fly in and out, long-tailed monkeys scamper about, from supporting beams a girdle of dangling gold leaves and carved dog bodies juts, inviting me to add my own to the monstrous pile. All this squatting, sway-backed feminine splendor is capped by a red-and-gold roof from the top of which a facelike gong glows amid white pennants. Then, rising out of the gong, a flashing *dorje* scepter.

Is it the hope this scepter can be mine that impels me, lying on my back, to send my eyes higher than they have ever strained? The top roof gleams with golden nodes that quiver with each shake and toss of my head. As I rattle them, I see the pagoda becoming more rotund, more femininely squat. A bell twanged, a lidded prayer cask rotated, what matter! Or all matters, because I now see the entire pagoda as the answer to my hands, my rushing, river-white breath. "At the entrance to everything I, Narayana, shall instill the world." What each of us desires, imagining nasturtium paste gilding the naked, sky-open temple of our body. Around our heads the raft of cobra hoods, tongues uplifted, wants more—more fire, more sky. To be roasted, sucked up, delivered unto. Night, rose water, hands, all that the pagoda brings, is: dove-lavenders I slip into, as into an avenue all shadow and column lined in a kingdom beneath the waves. I am darker, my temples glow with a whole ringing forest of song that, taken to bed, girds me in the roses her lips will usher forth, day broken, smiling.

On the eve of the trek, thinking of the mountains where Terror will shortly ride his wheels over me, I am still. Lost for many seconds, I am still. If my hands flutter like prayer flags, my tongue doesn't follow. Absorbed, all is absorbed: moon, fishes, and this God-sent earth. All this dreams. It has never been and neither have I, I think, looking across the road at a temple similarly entranced. Oh, for a word of light to breathe motion into massive stone curlicues! Far from that, my sandals breathe, contained rather than radiating. I would like to put on a fisherman's gown, dance with Shiva's eyes into flame. But I can't, anymore than I can lift my eyes to what is within me, growing. Instead I must quietly tilt back my head, hope another day's radiance finds me once more within it.

————————

Were my fears exaggerated? I was only going on a walk, not some perilous clinging to a rock ledge. But walks in the Himalayas inevitably carry a spiritual tinge, and the mountains were of an unrelinquishing grandeur; every time I lifted my eyes, I felt exalted. Yet walking was painful, the result of a knee cartilage I had unknowingly torn a few months earlier.

My knee might not have acted up without the sneaker-boot combination I affected after the first day. I had taken a wrong turn at virtually the first tree fork. By the time I had caught up, my hurrying, in boots that weren't broken in, had blistered one of my heels.

In the circumstances it made sense of a sort to combine a sneaker with a boot. While the sneaker probed, the turtlelike boot could smash fearlessly ahead. Between them I felt proof against most eventualities. But I hadn't reckoned on what the height difference would do to my spine, since the sneaker had to proceed on tiptoe to keep abreast of its giant companion. Eventually my knee began to react to my footwear strategies, just as I had reacted to our sixty-person-strong expeditionary force. That was what had gotten me lost: wanting to get ahead of the barefoot, tubercular crowd of porters, each with 120 pounds of gear strapped to his forehead. After a sharp climb from the road in the equatorial sun, they were not what I wanted to be near. So I lit out, hoping to spot a few birds.

My bolt, which necessitated the dispatch of a Sherpa to find me, was my last. As we hurried back, he dunned into me the difference between a private stroll and a trek that had to make twenty miles a day in order to cross Tesi Lapcha Pass before the first monsoon rains arrived.

With the loss of freedom came a sense of purpose, measured by how one kept pounding along. The porters did it superbly, whereas I, for all my soccer, was clearly in trouble. Everything aimed toward a zenith: the pass, the campsites I strove to reach. With that sustaining purpose I walked, envious of the Sherpas, those human chimes so cheerfully serene, their faces even when bowed reflecting their pleasure in being part of the circulation of light, wind, river, and stones.

I am speaking about the half hour late I daily limped in. For others, progress may have been less illuminating than this *will I* or *won't I* tapped on every rock face. But I suspect what I felt was abnormal only in its hobbling intensity. Signs of consideration for the wayfarer were legion: in inscribed *mani* stones; in a promontory's slate-engraved seats; in a hard, bright-green leaf holding out a hillside's trickle like a hand. In a world where all activity is regarded as spiritually endangering, we human trucks need all the *stop, look,* and *listen* signs we can get. So, when in the middle of a path a *mani* stone appears, take it, British-style, on your right. And mutter something, *"Om mane padme hum"* ("May the jewel blast in your name, Lord, evermore").

If the walking was hard, the mornings were signally beautiful. "Bright knocks to blue kingdoms make mountains," I'd exclaim, astonished at apparitions that seemed cut out of cardboard: in blue sky, a vertical of leaping white. I felt contained, as if walking inside a great pot. "That tree," I'd note, "is on my left and the light swoops across it like a hawk." But two hours later,

I'd be hard pressed to tell one tree from another. Everything had become a crashing glitter where each mica flake struck a para-noiac note.

Why not stop, sit down for a moment, and relax. How else remember?

By thinking about it, thinking "train in the night"; an ever stretching (or was it receding?) human chain swinging me by one foot, now the other. "Nothing is around me," I'd tell myself, trying to concentrate. When, at a bend in the path, a forager ap-peared, eyes welling forth in greeting, I kept walking. In a land-scape of stones, the trekker becomes a stone himself, concerned only with stepping over, around, and by stones. Finally a mo-ment came when I would have to sit down, busy myself with my thermos, less for the water than the respite opening the rucksack provided. "I am reaching to the head of the stair," I'd find myself mumbling, back on my feet. "I have nowhere to go—but up."

Around me wind circled a dry-mouthed desperation. Maybe some red-beaked choughs ash-floated by. Or a red beetle ap-peared at lap height, not far from a patch of orange moss. Every-thing else shrank to modicums of breath, to knowing I must once again stop, find for my eyes a shadowy crevice in which to tunnel.

My exasperation focused on the dearth of *presence*. But where mountains absorb so much, what else has a chance?

———————

Much of my rancor vanished with lunch, invariably celebrated under trees, by a clanging, sun-lidded stream. Afterward legs felt like good stout planks again, ready to walk wherever the chain should take me. "More up-going, down-going," a kitchen porter teased as he prepared to dash on ahead, to have tea ready when we arrived.

"Stop-going," I felt like replying, irked by the lack of levelness in valley-straddling paths.

Then the first breezes would begin to stir, and terraced, chest-high cornstalks waved where I prodded myself down, along, in the fastness of late shadows.

Where everything must be carried from *up* to *below,* and from *below* back to *up,* there is no reason not to be slow, white hat on head, teeth glittering in the chastening wind.

———

A constant mystery, as we picked our way from one valley to the next, were the steps hewn in rock faces. By whom it was done I can't imagine, for I never saw a man, hatchet in hand, on a path. Most of those we passed were foragers, usually boys and girls in their late teens. There was one such party who, for the whole of an afternoon, walked beside a friend and me. Every now and then they made us stop and offer a match. One had a harmonica, the others lips and mouths. They kept insisting we dance for them. On a rain- and wind-washed promontory we obliged, shifting scarves to a two-step. Then they picked up their round barrows and hastened on. At each succeeding viewpoint there they would be, ranged in a circle around the harmonica, waiting. This passing and repassing of their smiles and loads of cut wood made me feel both quickened and anxious, like a person in a car trying to stay abreast of a sunset.

The mountaintop Sherpa villages we camped by were always a surprise. "Where will they have hidden it this time?" I wondered as, far behind, I climbed through a forest toward Bedding, a thirteen-thousand-foot-high village where we were to spend three days acclimatizing before attempting to cross Tesi Lapcha, an eighteen-thousand-foot-high pass. I was convinced I was lost when I stumbled upon huts of a type new to me, their black, padlocked stone eerily contrasting with mounds of ghostly prayer flags. But this site of weird rites and evil mutterings (mine in the dripping mist-rain-snow of the near night) was a mere foraging center, and I trudged upward through thinning trees. Finally at a small pass I heard a whistle. It was the cook Passang, who had kindly walked out with a thermos of sugared tea to wait for me.

I asked Passang where the village was. He pointed in the direction of some rushing water.

A half hour later we arrived. The faces of children jumping about brush fires in their leggings and thin shirts looked like something right off the moon: round, orange cheeked, and very happy, as if everything, now that we had found them, was going to be all right. Teeth chattering like children at a beach, they surrounded us, wanting to show us everything: houses, various jewels they took off one by one for us to admire. But it was cold and I couldn't stand around like their mothers did, warming my hands in the hidden softness of armpits.

Rather than see us disappear, they decided to accompany us to our campsite twenty minutes upriver. They were good guides, knowing exactly where all the stream crossings were, having arranged the stones for hop, skip, and jump leaps. As I walked behind, it struck me why some people might prefer not to settle in slow-moving river valleys, among mounds of fertile clay. Playgrounds are of necessity bleak: the other side of the railroad tracks, the school dump.

So much defies description, like the black-on-black of a crow passing over granite. Or the crackle of laughter as our guides' tent flap lifts to a flash of creviced faces, *tsampa*-licking fingers, rakish caps. The caps roof an Asian imperturbability as they squat waiting for the guffaw that will bring them alive, that is so specific as to have the effect of a curtain slammed down. Then the chatter resumes, words glimmering against foreheads' intense oak. Faces are open and copper shiny, but so grained they seem porous, caves to edge fingers along, with stalactite teeth out of which the explosion of laughter will burst all jagged like an inundating sun.

———————

Next morning, the village is out, so sparkly by a gray, glacial silt river as to seem, for a brief moment, a city rather than a mere twenty houses. These are single-story dwellings, scattered so there is always a walled field to ensure privacy. Not that the Sherpa has much to hide. The only door is the entrance, shut more for reasons of wind than to keep people out. There, on a bed of straw, sleeps the yak, great horns and fluffy coat glistening out of the gloom. The rest is an earthen-floored room, its central fireplace set off by ankle-high rails—to keep kitchen coals in and sleepers out.

The houses cannot be described as comfortable. Round field stones are hard to build with, and the valley wind whistles in through fittings of straw and mud. For lack of a chimney, or windows, everything is a fire-begrimed black, perfectly at one with yak, goat, rock, and crow.

As I traipse about, a few colors emerge: pied markings of hopping, round-horned sheep; red- or orange-tipped bracken bordering a bright-pebbled stream; maroon dresses dining on potatoes in a subzero field. While across the black spectrum, to a purposeful ricochet of plinking stones, float the cloudlike shapes of a pair of yaks.

Above the village, hidden by a screen of pines, stands a *gompa,* or temple. Like churches of old, the *gompa* is a seat of joyful noise. How much loudness does worship demand? In ringing notes comes back *"Om mane padme hum,"* not "the jewel in the lotus" so much as a river flowing through a mountain gorge. A fine din they make as I stumble in to a rattling of bells and braying ten-foot-long trumpets. A stuffed, snarling tiger head guards the front altar decorated with colored streamers and a miniature regatta of lit yak-butter candles. The lamas all wear watches. As they bend over scores, their breaths fog their spectacles. Each is his own frog, his own painted gargoyle. Blue knocks to white kingdoms bring not only dawn but laughter too.

In Bedding we dismiss our barefooted porters, hiring in their stead the local villagers—every able-bodied man and woman we can find, a monk included. We then tramp up to the summer pasturage of Gurung, where we spend another day acclimatizing. Then comes our hardest day, over glacial moraine to the foot of Tesi Lapcha.

Morning dawns to ladders of mist, gray snow patches, here and there a large inscribed boulder, like a heron, creating depth. The ground is recent granite debris. As I advance my gliderlike bulk, feet seem chasms away, mouth a star. Gravitational pull I teeter over, never sure when a rock will blast up like a woodcock.

As day warms, streams loosen ice bonds, fanning out in marble-toy transparencies. Or a pond appears, drops of gold in a vault sliced white by wind. In the heat mirage, thousands of plovers wheel like something out of a bubble machine. Then their surprised, querulous voices vanish before our tips, veers, crashings.

Twice on overhangs porters separate from their loads. While our standard of living is retrieved, we stand about, afraid even to talk for fear of launching an avalanche. Yet without such halts, I'd be left far behind, unable to perform the shifting, rock-to-rock scamper moraine requires. Not helping is my sneaker-boot combination. But my first-day blisters haven't healed and I can't risk reopening them a day before Tesi Lapcha.

At a glacier lake we meet a walking store: a Japanese mountaineer who, for the past eight days, has been climbing the peaks of the Tesi Lapcha glacier. His scarred face shows he has not had an easy time. His most recent fall, he tells us, came on the tricky descent into our valley. His pack must weigh as much as he. Those with a predilection for ice picks and ropes load up. Then the brave man leaves and I find myself in tears. If getting down was so hard for him, what will the climb be like for us?

We dine at sixteen thousand feet amid falling snow that heralds the arrival of the monsoon. Our preparations now carry a moonlike artificiality, from the kerosene we cook with to the doubled gloves in which we attempt to eat. A friend's worsening cough (each upward step a rasp) has our doctors worried. But with only a day's kerosene left, we must cross Tesi Lapcha or face an eight-day detour.

We rise next morning in the dark, so many pieces of stamping, shivering expectation. For the second time only, I don my great boots. Everything else I stuff in my duffel bag; let the porters thump around under it!

The whistle: breakfast! Tea, peanut butter, hot porridge, to which I add all the salt and sugar I can. Parkas, gloved fingers chat above a board's plastic stools.

In prospect is a long tramp across the valley floor to where the climb proper starts. With my questionable knee I want us to be off early while the snow is still firm. I see the climb as an issue of so many feet, and so much daylight to complete it in. While we loiter, bag lunches are issued, each with a chocolate bar and five sugar pills. Finally, at a signal from the head Sherpa, we set off, tramping across a silt of night-fallen snow. Across the valley, moon-white mountains glow, an eeriness broken here by an avalanche's massive powdery rumbling, there by a frozen waterfall's turquoise shimmer of dripping arrows. Occasions to halt, let out breath to a night earth held in sky's containment, where the walker is himself but mist, tomb in a valley, hope under a cloud.

At the end of the valley, a hill's red-and-tan boulders. Coughing, heads rising, shoulders pulling, we mount—hand over fist over rock over eye—in a light that seems almost solid, something I could take an ax to, carve out a silhouette—me, blue parka fitted to bright stone slab.

After a slippery ax-cut traverse midway up comes a steeper climb along the inner edge of a cliff. The threat, however, is less of a fall than of being conked by a stone dislodged by hands and knees scampering above. The climbing I find exhilarating—an adult-size tree with no branches to poke out an eye. Availing myself of those forgotten appendages, my arms, I haul myself up and up to find myself in a snow bowl among a group of shuffling porters.

How, for all their lack of heeled boots, the porters find cliff holds, I don't know, but hold they do, trampling the snow with black, red, and green snowshoes. Tongues protrude and heads shake as they walk. The rest is heels, heels, a walking densely pronged with earth: necks bowed, goggled eyes, a big crate borne on the back like the proverbial calf.

As each mounts, his body, spread under its burden, floats turtlelike in round hieroglyphic waves. I can't tell whether it's head or eyes, but something bulges, sways, shifts with each thrust of his arms, blue weighted against his shirt. As he moves, his shadow envelope stiffens; each stab forward almost requires an act of levitation, a dispersal of light from shoulders to knees as they wedge along. A shuffling canal. A black weight. A star.

How strange to walk large as a burst flower across the still expanse. Emerging over a bowl new as the moon, a mast-tall shadow steers me, in luminous brocade chasing a sunlit harp. Have I ever seen air purer? Jade glacier pits; blue icicle nails clinging to black granite. The gloves rowing at my sides, my stranded, fishlike gulpings for breath all give a feeling less of terra firma than of a diamond city fetched from beneath the waves.

With such beauty there has to be a catch. At the top of a knoll, it comes, a wind blast straight in the face. Rather than be torn apart, I decide to back into it like a horse. A bit ludicrous, I can tell from those passing, but eventually I arrive at some jagged outcrops where others are already seated like gophers, munching away.

While we lunch, Sherpa ice cutters fan out across from us on a vast north-facing slope, orange knots of breath on our final ascent.

But the wind that has made a treadmill of walking veers around and, by sheer updraft, hoists me along in a way I might never have managed on my own. All I have to do is to turn out my toes, let flop the parka sails of my arms, and the blast does the rest, pushing me along as one might a loaded cart.

As if from some invisible zone below, crate-bearing porters zigzag along orange lines. I watch them stopped in a huddle to gossip. But there remains little time to dally as I plod upward five, seven steps at a time, reflecting cliffs underlining the "White Ice Makes Heron Grim" I imagine blazoned in pennantlike letters across my scraping, hacking chest.

Burrow my way up, how? With claws, comes back the answer, as I press one foot over the other in a needle-bright pace where wind seems the sole remaining instigator. "Won't be long now," says every smile in every fire-stained face looking down to encourage us drooped, lordly ones sunken in the snow as if never able to rise again. I look at the angel carpet of their boots. I look at their wide-set begoggled eyes. "May nothing hurt them," I pray.

By now my eyes are burning, my feet are stakes I must struggle to uproot, while the wind blasts an electronic howl and each stride matches shadow's ramifying gloom. But when I can't see in the swirl to push a foot forward, not ten feet away, fluttering choughs pipe red-beaked encouragement—and in a little while I've gained the ice-coated summit.

The wind howl at the top is such that merely watching our guides springing about on an overhang like foxes has me in tears. Exuberance so surpassing my own! But the ice makes for a slippery descent. Twice, rope lines must be set up. Even then, the valley is atumble in runaway crates. With boots, it seems easier—arms spread, heels together, hopping, a bird dipping in lilting drops through a snowscape. Unfortunately, not air boned. Twice, near the bottom, I crash through. On a snowless moraine we pitch camp.

———————

By contrast, the two-day walk down to Tamu and along its river to our guides' hometown of Khumjung seemed positively alpine. Paths clothed us in conifers. The field walls were knee-high. A stream sparkled gingerly between my sneakers, blue dwarf iris lining its bank.

While most flowers awaited the coming monsoon, rhododendrons were in full bloom: sixty- to one-hundred-foot-high crimsons, pinks, bridal whites. This is trekking, I thought, as I halted by a plank or imagined myself, a traveler in another age, being drawn across in a pulley basket. With no need to hurry, I could sit above a bank's stone-buried canoes, watching a rapid. Whirling feathers, circles, composed the thin, scattered roar of a morning spent sitting on a few rocks in a lost valley.

Then the pattern swept by and, when I looked again, *I* was annulled: an unencircled spot in the on-swirling eddy. I could *see,* but I could not *be;* not both at once. I had to understand this impossibility as if my future depended upon it. Here was no Arcadian garden but a river valley's acute, distressing angles asking me to open myself to the challenge of a life perpetually maintained in the blast.

To study in a cliff-hung Tamu River monastery, how tempting—did not part of me suspect the problems of communal integration, this *I, you, they, us,* flailing about in unconjugable counterdirections? However, I did use my knee as an excuse to forgo a second trek up to Everest base camp and spend instead a few days camped in a forest clearing below the celebrated Tyangboche lamasery.

With the cutting of the Tibetan trade route, the lamasery had fallen on hard times. To make up for the lost revenue, the lamas had businesses: a Coke and hotdog business, an antiques business, a greasy wood- and parchment-engraving business. All this polluted. The lamas hurled paper cups under the trees. The Everest trekkers threw their used toilet paper there. Who was to pick it up?

We, of course, with our humbly tendered baskets. In honor of its reincarnate *rinpoche,* new trash pick-up signs were lettered and approved, then posted at offending sites.

If I failed to participate in the Everest trek, I did make the most of the lamasery forest. At fourteen thousand feet the eye had aisles to wander in, their white bark marking a quiet in which I heard my own fevers, silklike, dripping. Birds abounded, tiny rainbow fragments spun from the surrounding mist-prism. Pride of place went to the reigning national emblem, a pheasant with a peacock-blue tail patch at the end of enormous orange-flashing wings. Almost as rare was a grouse, gray as a bobcat save around the eyes, pink within swirls of red. One late afternoon as I waded in a meadow of twisting rivulets, from the middle of a pine tree I was greeted by a loud moist silvery call: a gray fly-catcher, I saw, with a long red pennant of a tail. On alighting, it revealed a cap of an unearthly sky blue juxtaposed against an orange belly. There, admiring him, one rock among the many, I sat for as long as the twilight lasted, binocular fingers shivering in the mist. Greedy, greedy.

We had returned from Tyangboche to Khumjung when, on our next-to-last day, we decided to take in the Saturday market at Namche Bazaar, two thousand feet below. In recent years Namche had received a certain fame as the assembly point for

Everest expeditions. For highlanders of the Khumjung-Tamu region who raised only potatoes and onions and the odd yak for food, a market was essential. (How much so was shown by the willingness of traders to walk in from as far as ten days away.) For one without the time to take in the whole of the region, here was a chance, by descending a few thousand feet, to catch something of its tribal variety.

In a jiffy, a joint lit, here I am tumbling out of my tent for the climb up the ridge. A bit silly when, halfway up, I discover I've forgotten my hat. The hole being bored in my skull may be no more than a flute hole wide. But at fifteen thousand feet, with the sun screaming like an eagle, I don't want to be a target, traipsing along where pine trees dip and black earth fissures away in golf-ball curves. In the distance, mountains loom as always, unfailingly grand, smoke-silver earth aquachromed in startling blue. Excuse to squat on an outcrop while a stunted tree draws in bristles of shade, a chough hovers in the distance.

On the far side of the ridge, past the tin cans of a new airstrip, a sharp plunge has me gingerly lowering myself on elbows from rock to rock. Suddenly a roar wafts up, so loud I burst out laughing.

"There!" a companion shouts, pointing to a hillside's tin-flashing roofs. But between glare and ground fog, I can't make out a thing. Giggling, shaking my head, I hurry on, wondering what compels me to behold rings within voices within stars, the market's crashing cataract of match-quick humanity.

A few more hops on the rock trail and Namche bursts from under the fog. A lone spruce towers over a triple row of houses lifted alive by lines of spanning white flags. To a second hill clings the market: pinks and reds of women's sweaters firecrackle against earth and skirt blacks like so many Seurat disks.

I am noting these impressions when I hear what seems to be my name being hailed. Easy thing to spot on a hillside, this Robin, and for a moment I pause, reluctant to leave my perch for a commercial circus. But rather than stay writing "red within red within red makes gold," I scramble on down, past chang houses and mud lanes lined with Tibetan antique traders—each presiding over a miniature city of relics—and on to the buzz of voices of the market hill.

Getting up on the cordoned-off marketplace presents something of a problem. I pass the one gateway where everyone is scampering up on all fours with a guffaw. It's only after I have made a complete round that I realize I have no choice but to get down, too.

Can five hundred angels trade on the head of a pin? A more Himalayan market would be hard to imagine, I think, as a human conveyor belt sweeps me along a row of squatting Sherpas with pitted, butter-glistening faces and hair braided like that of American Indians. Everything is negotiable; to the impersonal displays of cereals, kukri daggers, and carpeted bric-a-brac must be added all that jangles from neck, belt, wrists, and ears. Long skirted, thin waisted, in their dress complete as crows, they are the jewels they wear—jewels that start in the earth as fire and crystallize on the breast.

Not long before I, too, am squatting among them with my surplus Western treasures: high-altitude goggles, boots, pack, gloves. Around me foot-shuffling gems bustle along, grinning and counting, counting and grinning. How much for an elephant soldier mounted in wet silver? Or a pair of red, green, and black Sherpa boots?

By now the afternoon mists, harbingers of the coming monsoon, have begun to add to the selling urgency. Lacking adequate clothing, peddlers need to make warmer ground by nightfall. By 3 P.M. the market is nothing but blowing debris. In the lanes only Tibetans are left, wildly necklaced, with jewel-dangling ears and maybe a powder-blue cowboy hat, each rising out of his carpeted incense as I pass.

Outside the chang house a blue of electric fog marks houses, peering out of rock shells. On a knoll I perch, wondering what the mist will snatch next. Here, high up, the valley narrowness comforts. I think I understand what choughs are up to, flying from point to point of redness, rock.

Back into the tavern for more chang. Coppery gonglike faces gleam above the wall bench. Trays before them, mostly bare. A black, fire-stained peace. The chang bowl is drunk, then washed, and perhaps another tries its wide, heron-inscribed mist. No one talks. Sweeping hands, wind-red faces. Now and then a boy blows, flutelike, into a double-tiered grate where tea and potatoes steam.

I step out, into a blackness so transparent the quarter moon suffices to light the line of a path stretching past farms and bare fields. Everything seems to be waiting. I feel very thin, alone, joyful.

Beginnings of a Life Abroad: Two Houses in the Burgundian Auxois
1973–1978

I had gone to Nepal as the first stage in a projected journey through Southeast Asia. But I had lost a lot of weight in the mountains, and efforts to put it back in the restaurants of Kathmandu only brought me to the verge of dysentery. Rather than give up and go home, I decided to use my return ticket to stop off in France—a good place, one would think, to fatten up. Virgil and Anne Burnett had offered me the use of their house in the walled Burgundian mountain village of Montarnis. Little could I have guessed that the use of their house would soon lead to one of my own.

When I arrived in the second week of May, it was still wintry. But it made me appreciate each slightly warmer day all the more. As I walked about in the way Nepal had taught, taking in where I had landed, everything began to bud, including my writing.

It might be thought that the neighboring places I walked or drove to—Hauteroche, Saint-Seine-l'Abbaye, the pink granite fortress of Sémur-en-Auxois—exerted a compelling fascination. But the more I roamed, the better I understood how everything in the Auxois radiated inward to Montarnis. It was on the heights overlooking Vercingetorix's fortress of Alésia that Julius Caesar prepared the battle plan that was to make him emperor and impose Latin as the new world language. A thousand years later, from a rampart overlooking the same valley, Bernard of Clairvaux and Saint Louis of France dreamed up the first Crusade; all the more appropriate, as the poet Chateaubriand noted, because the site of Montarnis so resembled that of Jerusalem.

During the Middle Ages Montarnis became the religious center of the Burgundian empire. Its prosperity encouraged a rash of building—noblemen's palaces, mercantile counting houses.

In the centuries of neglect that followed, much of its patrimony tumbled into rubble, and Montarnis became once again the three-hundred-person subsistence-farming community it had been when Caesar camped there. But as I poked about among the ruins, I experienced something of what eighteenth-century painters had come upon in the Roman forum: cows stabled among one or two remaining columns; a ruin, perhaps, but still responsive to the touch of light.

Normally we see only the flesh of a town. Here, bared in chalky, luminous transparency, was its skeletal soul.

Just as Montarnis was a ruin, a folly, as gardeners say, so was the Burnetts' house. Some might have fixed it up, tossed out the straw mattresses and aluminum pots it came with and installed modern plumbing and drains, a phone, a television set. But not Virgil and Anne. Apart from an FM radio—to catch the indispensable *France Musique*—the house remained basically what they had bought a little more than ten years earlier. The past, they knew, creates us, and the last thing they wanted was to disturb festering antiquity, mushrooms growing out of bathroom walls, fountains erupting from the third-floor ceiling after a storm. They had bought the house for its fireplaces and the stories Montarnis might yield. The house enshrined a sense of imaginative possibility, and they were not about to louse it up with needless lamps and fuse boxes, drains, tiles, and all the rest of it. Let it molder away! And the mushrooms on the bathroom walls—what better site!—could be greeted each year like old friends.

During my first six weeks in Montarnis, I was mainly occupied in describing my recent trek in Nepal. And something about the test I had undergone must have evoked the joy I registered in my little notebook jottings. Here was another hilltop world, but so much greener. Day by day, I found myself more and more alive.

———

Uncertainties pass. I shiver as if I hold in my numb fingers all my wounds, then watch helplessly as I see them taken away, swollen. "No one ever admits anything," I mutter, applying notions of peasant reserve to the carriage yard's dormant garden. But then doesn't everything real require, like frost, a melting inward? Bursts of paper, iron flies of sunshine welling overhead.

In the morning there is jam and coffee. "Blue tongue from a rooster's crow," I write, leaning out from a window over the cobbled lane below. "Light it, day!"

In response comes a blackbird whistle corkscrewing upward as if to announce there is sky about, a vibrant electric blue against which eaves and chimneys gleam like giant whale fins.

Below, day, aboil in the chimney, stokes its pot. A thermometer writes away for sun. The hour turns. To a cake of soap near a soap dish, a head of lettuce by a pan.

Outside, quiet carts trundle down the lane. A farmer holds a wheelbarrow by one hand as he prods it through the barn door. Beyond his pegged jacket, shaft figured in dim light, a horse, attached to a post like a spring to a door. The silences move so they glisten: nail from which I remove my book, let a beaten blade of sunlight tap me into mild surprise. A wish rising from a well. An arrow of midnight, alone.

———

In a long May twilight, how lovely to walk and watch lilacs turn from gray to amethyst to an almost tourmaline pink. Or to come upon a bunch of pansies proposing—a night among themselves, all furs and crinolines dancing. Lobelias tumble from a wall in sky-blue cascades. Along the roadway, forget-me-nots form clusters of chalk-blue mist, risings of earth into the nettle banks among which they shyly rustle, all the while stamping their tiny feet.

Golden silver hour. In the glaze, stockings of sky mount green hills to infinity. Martial and clear stand the rampart dwellings, their slate roofs almost liquid in red, clouding air.

Any twilit lane, with its geranium hues of stone and shadow, submits me to a world where color is speech, a series of points flickeringly scattered. The sky seems to hold it longer, from the initial yellow-mauves to the last filaments of red. To such fixity I can give myself, sitting entranced under transformations of cloud into something more like taffeta or satin in still, shiny air.

To the countryman, that blue-denimed creature of the vine, with his pink cheeks and red smokestack nose, Plato's cave argument scarcely holds. For it is not sun, but a mottled panoply that lies outside stone-bound fields. Where the Mediterranean sees a duel of light and shade, the Burgundian thinks contours, a lip-nipple here, a bosomy curve there, each replete like a pâté in its jellied form.

For him a sunset becomes a Rubensian flesh-forest, alive in each pink hole and escaping vapor: dragons of the moon; breathing hulks and spitting fires; a salon where men in wigs bow their heads, their wills.

Would that such a sky might teach me to honor woman for her very excesses, the pearls carrying a throat, the dispersal of everything to a brown bush by a blue star.

For it is this, back in my bedroom, my windows dance with: pink effulgence brightening to roseate flame; crooking a finger around her waist and smiling, all is now so thick, so clear where the sky is my lid and the blue envelope sinks in, nightlier than

ever. Moon, I see now, rises, stippling the night with still shat-
terings, clothed softnesses, a door between, a first star quieting
violet electric air.

———————

I was able to stay in Montarnis only until mid-June. But I returned as soon as the Burnett house became vacant again in September. I was a city boy who had always wanted to live in the
real countryside. If one spring had taught me so much, what
would the remaining round of a year yield? It was that com-
pleteness I wanted to experience.

Much of my satisfaction had to do with the rural time clock
in which, like a mouse, I now found myself. Each time I got off
the train from the city I was struck anew by how quiet the villages were, lost in the trees and the blue smoke-mist of surrounding valleys.

Back home we Americans have won our war with nature.
Roads, dams, metal bridges, and shopping malls, all that achievement resonates. In a countryside where buildings and walls are
made out of stone—porous limestone, at that—and roads are
more like rivers than great straight marching lines, the combat
of nature and civilization has been more equal. One is not in a
world of engineers, as one is across the Swiss border, but in one
of peasants, people who still move by nature's clock. The brusque
changes of weather, the steepness of the narrow valleys, the frac-
tured holdings—a wood here, a field or an orchard there—do
not encourage rational farming. "Amputate it! It's not econom-
ical!" consumer nations cry, unable to imagine a life where shoppers are not in full command. To some extent, they have pre-
vailed. By 1950, the rural trades had mostly vanished, but there
were many peasants still hanging on.

In Montarnis, the battle against their extinction was still being waged. In the same spirit with which protesters elsewhere sat

in, marched, and hurled themselves before trains, here foreigners—mainly artists and writers—pitched in, doing what they could to keep an ancient way of life from disappearing when there was still much to be learned from it.

We think of peasants as humble folk. In reality, they are snobs—and with good reason, since the food, the wine, and much of what we think of as French originates with them. Their values are distinct. A case in point was a local woman who had been running a one-room grocery out of her home for twenty years. All this time she had been selling peppers.

"They're very good," she tells me, reassuringly.

But has she ever tried them? I ask, wondering.

"Of course not," she replies, "they're not from here." And I understand immediately what a betrayal it would be for her to put a few slivers in a salad.

Theirs might be a subsistence culture, but I had only to attend a single picnic, or poke around in an attic, to see that by any standard I knew, they lived very well. To be sure, getting to know peasants was a problem. The very nature of their work made for a closemouthed, reserved people. But the posttractor, postchainsaw depopulation of the countryside could leave room for an extra pair of hands, or even eyes. And in an ancient village where the families all hated one another, a stranger had value as a go-between.

The aid I offered was certainly slight. During the wine harvest I helped pick grapes, toiling up the slope behind my neighbor's vigorous eighty-year-old father, one of the few who still possessed an alcohol permit. Since the family could not justify owning a car, I became their chauffeur, driving whoever needed to catch a train to the railroad station in the next valley in exchange for a generous amount of potatoes or a few bottles of Pinot.

For intellectual company, there were other expatriates. To a man, they were artists with a small *a,* not out to invent themselves anew but to restore respect for craft, for the mystery of calling. If the past is reality, why not employ it as an actual setting for one's fiction, a source of costume for one's erotic drawings? Why not master perspective, the art of the *veduta,* and make a living as a trompe l'oeil muralist? Every couple of weeks we would meet one-on-one, in a restaurant over lunch and a good bottle of wine.

To a man we shared an admiration for peasants: for their herbal medicines; for their cooking, an art with almost as great a range as the more celebrated *cuisine bourgeoise;* and for the lengths to which they went to assure that nothing they touched was ever wasted. In the Auxois in late winter one prunes cassis bushes. What does one do with the twigs—kindling? No, one scrapes off green buds and sells them to the pharmacist, who will grind them into a fine-scented powder, useful for storing linen.

Anyone who has driven around France knows how varied a land it is: each twenty miles offers virtually a new culture. In the Auxois not only is each valley different, but each village differs as well by whether it's up high or down on the road below, and by all that the centuries have built up, here a fountain, there a hermit's seat or a Roman-looking washhouse. The local art— dry stone masonry—ensured that I had something to think about wherever I walked. On every stroll I learned about what fits where and with what, and about a countryside where no two days ever seemed alike.

As week by week the spring carpet rose, each layer taller, different in its range of color from the last, the notion of staying on and putting down roots of my own began more and more to seem what I should do.

In my previous travels, I had always compared the new world I was taking in with the America in which I had been brought up. As a writer, I looked for air, for freedom, for prospects larger than the fear-drenched fifties in which I had come of age. But constant comparisons made for a divided self. However I tried to escape from them, I felt always pulled back by prior commitments: to my family, to a loved one, to what I saw as a career. I was perpetually torn between the expanded identity I experienced traveling and the reality in which I had to live. Finally, with Nepal and the climb over Tesi Lapcha, something snapped. There, on the far side of Tesi Lapcha, I realized that, after so many attempts, I was finally free. I could be my own master, beholden only to myself. I wanted to write a book about my escape, all those failed attempts. Why not do it where I was learning so much and felt, for the first time in my life, centered?

Unfortunately, I had already agreed to rent a cousin's house in Mendocino for the summer, as I needed a place to spend time with my two sons, who still lived in California. Once there, what was to keep me from succumbing to the temptation of a new woman or a new job? A man who has often felt seduced has to take precautions. Rather desperately, I began to cast around for something that would root me as an expatriate.

The thought of expatriating myself may have been romantic infatuation, but it was one for which I had spent much of my life preparing myself. Who, after all, *was* an American? Was *my* identity defined by place? By the vast expanse of possibility the continent offered? Or was it, as the eighteenth century thought, an openness to the new, to the changing instant we carried in us, part and parcel of our famous mobility?

To some such end, as a way of situating myself and providing a future choice, I had majored in American history and literature as an undergraduate. I wrote a senior thesis on American expatriation in the century preceding World War I to define what settling abroad meant. What were the bogeys that various generations of Americans feared? What were they looking for in France, Italy, England, the South Seas, Tokyo? And in themselves, in their own being as writers, as artists?

Was going abroad, recrossing the Atlantic, merely another "sea-change / Into something rich and strange?" A chance to masquerade as members of a more theatrical, more artistic milieu? Or did crossing the waters, that "death by drowning," involve something far deeper: a descent into the mythic underworld in search of knowledge, power, an artistic birthright? Something that would allow them to rise above the accident of nationality and take on a more universal significance? An American, yes, but also a citizen of the globe, a world poet, an Orpheus. Expatriation could be an act of artistic self-transformation.

———

While living in Montarnis, I played soccer for the team of a nearby town that specialized in train repairs. It solved, as my teammates put it, the problem of Sunday. And it gave me a way to orient myself among the cow pastures of western Burgundy, where my spikes probed cheeselike consistencies of village muds: runny *Epoisse,* stinky *Chaource.* Soccer brought a social identity and friends with different aspirations from those of the Montarnis peasants. For the game, half the town would turn out, noses red from Sunday dinner. Afterward we'd all convene at a café. My loneliness, my need for company, were sufficiently assuaged.

In May, at the end of the soccer season, we had our annual banquet: even by Burgundian standards a substantial affair, with ten full courses and wine pouring into any glass with so much as a lip exposed. After a further round of stories and joke telling, everyone danced to a violin and accordion played by two of our mates.

By five in the morning, I was sated. After shaking hands with everyone as one must, I lurched to my car only to discover, as I backed out over a steeply cobbled curb and smashed up the rear axle, that I had no brakes. A volley of cheers swept the restaurant as I stepped inside, and the team captain undertook to drive me home, every cylinder blasting at full throttle through impenetrable fog.

I awoke a while later to a sky of such deep, unearthly blue that I had no choice but to grab pen and notebook and go for a walk. This time I set out by a way new to me, through the arched postern gate on the other side of the village.

On a brisk morning, a walk becomes of necessity a cultivation of successive warmths, of sun-reflecting outcrops on which I perched as if carved from a piece of silver. As I peered at valley greens far below, elation shivered its flames like wind. To be sure, the little hilltop I was on, for all its beauty, hardly compared to Greece or Nepal. Nor was it even the region of France that most enchanted me. But I had put forth new roots of a kind. And, unlike Greece and Nepal, France had a culture that spoke to me. By comparison with anything I had known, the countryside seemed rich, with hourly changing sensations, presences, fragrances, all that old limestone cliffs and wooded hilltops cathedrally provided.

I felt so at home in Burgundy, what was the bogey I feared? For a writer, hearing one's own maternal language, that idiomatic raciness, counts inordinately. But I didn't want to be constantly bombarded with the latest commercial refuse. Living abroad, I was unlikely to become any the less American, and I would have the satisfaction of knowing a larger world.

In expatriating myself, I believed I could avoid the mistakes of the twenties generation. Perhaps in the Paris of that time, writing on a café's zinc counter may have offered its own distracted sense. But how much more meditative to squat on a steep, barely cart-sized path, noting a hilltop's descending rush of silences and light.

As I sat, watching a pair of crows harry a black kite, up the path came a herdsman to stroke the noon with his staff, his blue work shirt. How in almost a year in this three-hundred-person village had we never met? To make up for it, the two of us stood chatting away about the latest midwestern tornado until, with a sense of another piece of the village puzzle identified, we parted, he to his waiting family, I to whatever enchantment the valley still held out.

Downward, pointed on toes, I balanced, savoring the new snow whites, yellows, and blues among which I squatted and peered and sniffed. Was perfection a thick waxy pistil of bee-inviting sweetness, a meadow's unleafed willows arranged along a brook like so many upside-down harps? Among spring's presences, my uncertainties vanished.

Once on the valley floor, I began to circle back under a wire fence, past a late dogtooth violet and into a pasture lit with cowslip candelabras. Did I notice everything, was I still as a lake? For a moment, succumbing to the temptations of sun, I slumped, eyes shut on the grass, at peace. Then a hyacinth, last of its tribe, called, a blue star hoisted on a silky black stalk. Look for others? Yes, every orchestra wants new timbres. A few yards higher and I was no longer stepping carefully. A carpet is to walk on.

By now I had climbed where a brambled wall barred further progress. As I hesitated, a flash of leaf fire marked a crossing sparrow. A moment more and I had found the breach in the wall—but in no hurry, I postponed it, preferring the view from a three-stone altar.

As I took in the circuit I had climbed, it struck me that I could turn virtually any day into a like transparency, one that asked me only to look and try to absorb. Still, the textures were perhaps too privileged, too richly green. Eventually I might have to go to some cave at the top of an arid valley, where "Who am I?" might resolve into a man of boots and mountain peaks and sky. But for a newcomer, quickness charmed, open as I was to each trill, each mouth and hope and home. I wanted my hands to bear the autumn's long shattering descent of leaves as the landscape of blue turned to red, copper envelope, misted sun. To squat by shadowed moss while the distance welled with names: *nest, mouth of tremulous glass, wind's scissors cutting through pines.*

With that, I got up and stepped through the hedge hole where a gravel road invited. If Sherpas could live buoyantly in their high mountain fastnesses, why couldn't I in a countryside that so spoke to me?

———

To arm myself against further uncertainty, I needed to commit myself to staying where I was. One way to do it was to buy a house.

Montainis had a splendid one which I knew was available, a sixteenth-century merchant's house. Between two cornerstone turrets, a central tower staircase rose in front of five floors of spacious rooms with flagstone floors, enormous uncovered ceiling beams, and large carved windows. There was even a ninth-century Merovingian column in the cellar. From the balcony off the master bedroom you could see over the whole village and five adjacent valleys.

After a year of visiting, I was aware of what it lacked: no garden, no central heating, no chimneys; much of the masonry still awaited repairs (pigeons nested throughout the two top floors). Unlike the Burnetts' house, it required a good deal of renovation. I did not see myself as particularly suited to a baronial role. But I had run out of time and, panicking at the news of a prospective buyer arriving from Paris, I made the owner an offer.

No sooner was my handshake given and saluted in good burgundy than the real estate agent I had been dealing with called at my house. He had just found a wonderful property, a former doctor's house, in Vitteaux, some fifteen miles down the road toward Dijon.

But no, I told him, I wasn't interested, I had given my word and that was that.

Well, curiosity beckoned, and next morning, if only to see

the jewel I had missed, I found myself driving to Vitteaux, once a water-defended fortress town at the intersection of two well-traveled valleys. By chance, I turned off at a little bridge before the main street and asked people there whether a large property was, as rumored, for sale.

The house they directed me to lay opposite the lycée, on a rising street that at one time contained ecclesiastical buildings: church, convent, monastery, seminary. The outside, with its long plastered facade and firmly closed gray shutters, was anonymity itself. But throw open the heavy, multibolted oak door and you stood in Zeffirelli's *Traviata* set for the opening of act 2—an immense amber-tinted glass conservatory.

From beyond the conservatory invitations issued: toward the huge fireplace—false, of course—white Carrara marble complete with sculpted lion paws and a hearth screen bearing the arms of well-detested local barons. Or up a wide curving iron staircase lined with foot-high fossilized ammonites enclosing a grotto fountain. Or out through high glass doors into the walled garden's hornbeam allée with a view across the Brenne of hillside pastures.

The conservatory joined what were in effect two houses. The house on the left was tasteful Louis XV: no kitchen or bathroom, to be sure—Burgundians disdained baths—but there was a formal drawing room with a parquet floor, two enormous gilt mirrors set against walls of carved paneling, and in the corners, grisaille village scenes of a nocturnal spookiness.

A curving stone staircase set in the remnant of a medieval tower led up to a trio of bedrooms, each with painted paneling, sink, and marble fireplace. Up another flight, a stout beamed attic collected rainwater in a cement water tank for distribution to the bedrooms.

The nineteenth-century house on the opposite side of the conservatory revealed a more eclectic taste. A small library with a fireplace of serpentine marble issued, through a stained-glass entryway, into a pre-Raphaelite trophy room used as a doctor's office by the previous owners. It had, for privacy, its own stained-glass window, two elaborately carved doors adapted from an old wardrobe, and a wood-and-gilt mirror.

From the office, steps led down to a derelict kitchen, behind which a cramped staircase, of the kind one might encounter on a sloop, twisted up to a pair of elegant bedrooms. Down the garden steps and beneath the conservatory ran a vaulted wine cellar, with hooks for hanging meat and a labyrinth trap for dormice.

The grounds, gained from a pergola, were no less charming. A wall set with espaliered apple trees dropped me into an orchard and thence to a wood-and-clay Normandy-style barn with its own fishpond. From there a small driveway led through a great iron castle gate to the stone bridge where I had asked my way. Beyond the orchard wall, a trout stream ran under a dense cover of pines, oaks, and chestnut trees before disappearing into a fir wood that marked the end of the property.

My tour of the grounds up to the church cemetery and back along the overgrown eighteenth-century road with its elegant gate had taken a half hour. I now inquired the price, expecting a figure far out of my range. It was twenty-six thousand dollars, or ten thousand dollars less than what I was just about to buy. Size and attendant problems of upkeep had scared off local buyers. Still, it was perfectly livable.

There remained the matter of compensating the owner of the Montarnis house for the loss of the prospective buyer from Paris. (That house would change hands fifteen years later for eight hundred thousand dollars.) That done, I flew off to spend the summer with my sons in Mendocino. When I came back in September I was all alone. I remember a misty rain heralding an early winter. Below in my new orchard lay thousands of apples of a dozen varieties waiting to be picked. That night, after an afternoon spent on a ladder, I saw their reds and greens over and over again through closed eyelids. I knew I had been right to purchase the house.

Like anything neglected for eight years, the house required extensive work: new roofs and chimneys, a heating system, a kitchen and bathroom, and lots of repainting. Unlike the Burnetts in Montarnis, I had no choice but to remodel; and as might be expected, I made a number of mistakes. I stuck a bathroom in what should have been a formal dining room and put monster night storage radiators in the old bedrooms. I polluted the river with a pipe extension when, for the same cost, I could have built a septic tank. As for the drawing room, the starting point of any sensible restoration, I simply threw up my hands and left it the pretentious ruin it was.

Fortunately the town was an artisanal center. In the schoolyard across the road, children could be heard rehearsing the classic power games—"Fetch me this, run!"—eyes as bright with the fascinations of cement and power drills as mine had once been with bat and racquet.

To speed repairs, I engaged a trio of fourteen-year-olds who pretended to be experienced workers and certainly knew more than I about the waywardness of old stone. A friend sent for her brother, a carpenter. Little by little, within the limitations of my wallet, the house began to come alive. A landscape of cement waves—or was it mountains?—appeared in the skirting of the bathroom. I bought a café's soccer game for the conservatory and a pair of ewes with their lambs to mow the park and orchard. Inspired, the old piano teacher living across the street asked if she could contribute her own menagerie—a pair of nanny goats, a blind goose, three ducks, and a hen—and promptly retired to the local hospital.

To fence in the ewes and their ever escaping lambs I turned to Raoul Langeais, a burly, red-faced peasant from the Vosges who shared with a hideous crone half of a small cottage opposite my gate. Eventually, he came to spend most of his sober mornings working for me. Raoul liked working for me because I let him do as he saw fit and I didn't yell at him. In return, he imparted the lore he had picked up in sixty years of a very hard, alcohol-cursed life. Finally, though, his drunkenness reached the point where the crone told him he had to move out. Her husband, she claimed, had been released from his retirement home and needed Raoul's room. For a moment Raoul considered moving down the street to the hospital. He even walked there one evening intending to commit himself only to realize he could not face being incarcerated. With nowhere to go—I happened to be away at the time, or I could have put him up—Raoul took his shotgun, went into his cellar, and shot himself in the throat.

For most of the first year in my new house the novelty of what I was learning was enough to sustain me. But there were moments, walking past shuttered windows in the bitter blue of an evening, when I wondered what I was doing holed up in such a backwater. I could see that fixing up a house could become as preoccupying as a career had been years earlier. But did it have to mean burying myself where I would always remain an outsider? Wasn't my fundamental life concerned not with rural Burgundy but with America?

These thoughts did not go away. I was in my third May when one morning I found myself writing, "The metaphor of flying [that is, clearing out] is acute." If *flying* was so acute, what, I asked, changing the rhyme, of *lying?* At that I felt a surge of red, red vibrations beating where, as on an egg, I sat, sun shaved, typing. In a poem, perhaps, *flying* might be an Icarus released. Whereas now it brought merely a reminder of place closing in on me, that elongating frame of a summer's chores. What was to stop me from simply getting up from my desk, buttoning on a shirt, and leaving? My plants? My animals, those clocks forever sounding off in the fields?

Once again I feel the lure of travel, that notion of enlarging myself, bright face in the wind of a new culture. Outside the garden beckons, blue distances against hillside greens and red-roofed village stone. Why not walk out, drink in the gold of another May?

To a dream of shoes in wind, feet deposit me where an old stone bench mutes the park's disorder. Below, apple trees blossom, still so white! Grasses float high—to knee, waist. And branches sway down their shifting myopic peace. An unfinished work is a house thousands of stones old. I relish a stillness forever breaking, like rain out of fog, tempering my anxiousness with the sense of something quiet growing, snails among blue bottles of periwinkle.

Above me, pine cones form rich rust-velvet ascensions, like a peasant's corduroy jacket. The ground is stuffed with struggling density: "I'm the tallest," "No, I am," an argument among flowers, grass, and nettles. By a stream's floating greens I sit, a stocking filling against winter. The step under me is dry. *I will not go away.*

What is the wind doing? I rise, letting a hazelnut allée pull me where the eye touches distance, the hope and charm of sheep, hens, and roosters, planted things. Across the property wall a reaching tong of voices blends with river smoke and steam. I'm in a painting. Casual sunlight brings dew lace.

The other side of a little fir wood, Charolais cattle blossom like still cigarettes. Afternoon waves a diaper cloud. A settling crow sinks just out of sight into the orchard. I, too, have settled, buried the morning's misgivings in my hands. Rising through the pasture onto a plateau, a husk of moon lights my way. Slowly the moon folds me in its gravestones while, farther off, tomorrow's hills beckon, green slips of air. I liberate myself from silences. As I step, I am.

———————

For a couple of years, my resolution held. I knew why I was domiciled where I was. But one Sunday, while playing center-half on a sodden soccer field, I suffered a neck injury from heading too many balls. With much of my life ground to a halt—I couldn't even pull a rake—I began to question the rural project I had taken on.

The dwindling crossroads town in which I found myself did not encourage commitment. In the twenty-five years following the Second World War, Vitteaux had lost two-thirds of its population. Despite the parliamentary power wielded by a deputy mayor of the reigning conservative party, it would decline by another five hundred to a mere thousand during my five-year sojourn. This couldn't help but affect me. When a neighbor stretched forth a hand and invited me in, I often felt the desperation. Most of the townspeople had come to Vitteaux for the same reason as I—houses were cheap and with the savings they could start a small business. But houses are cheap for good reason, and walking past mournful gray-stone facades on a Poussin-blue winter evening, I could imagine myself in some forlorn backwater town. However breathtaking the views, or the distinction of a bridge, an old tower, a seignorial house, something ghostly made me question my motives for continuing to live there; all the more because my house relentlessly swallowed my income. "You could be paying for this the rest of your life!" my father had fairly shrieked on his one visit.

Argue though I did that it was not the house but the life it brought that counted, still, my father's burst of common sense registered. When my companion told me she wanted to move to a large English-speaking city, London or New York, where she could pursue a career, I was prepared to see her point. After all, I was a writer, and an English-speaking writer could not get the work he needed living in the remote Auxois. Given the choice of London or the New York I had hated as a child, I took her to one of those Scorsese movies, *Mean Streets* or *Taxi Driver.* After seeing it, she decided, very sensibly I thought, on London, and we left. As for the house, I sold it to the one professional who could make it work—a physician with his own equipment, who wanted to break the local doctors' monopoly.

Samarkand, Bukhara, Khiva
1988

SAMARKAND

Not so long ago, we judged civilizations by their cities. "Earth has not anything to show more fair," Wordsworth murmured, peering out from London Bridge. Nowadays, looking at the same view, it's not his "cloud-capped towers" we behold, but a version of Blake's "dark Satanic mills," where cars have become the instruments that chain us to a Satanic grid. For some, the object of travel still consists in a metropolitan city's emporiums, museums, theaters, and restaurants. But others of us would rather choose Bali or a trek in the Himalayas than "see Naples—and die." The city is no longer the absolute siren of old.

The notion of a planet where humans' constructions form a mere fraction of its ongoing glory may be salutary in the long run. But in the short run, it works against cities. If they are dying, it is, I suspect, less because of the blights we have unleashed than because we have lost Wordsworth's knack of seeing them as havens created from our aspiring selves, our eyes, our skin and bones.

Now and then an Italo Calvino succeeds in imagining cities afresh, each labyrinth more bewitching than the last. The rest of us may be condemned to travel—the farther, perhaps, the better. Out there, *east of the sun and west of the moon,* it may flash on us that *Eden* was simply a name for the first city. Oh, we say, seeing it through a desert traveler's eyes, so that's what a city was, paradise—old Persian for a "walled garden." Extend the garden walls far enough and you have a city.

Eden has long since vanished in the sands, but we can still feel something of its resonance if we travel to the great desert paradises of Central Asia—Samarkand, Bukhara, and Khiva. Not only were they centers of important civilizations, but they remain, even today, that increasingly rare thing, beautiful cities.

To us, cities are fixed, palpable creations, built of rock, not fine-blown glacial dust. Put one down and chances are it will stay there. Bruges may become Bruges-la-Morte when the North Sea withdraws, but it does not abandon its towers and canals to go chasing after receding water. In Central Asia, though, cities tend to lead a more spectral life. Stuck in a *back of beyond,* in an element that could be imagined as sky itself, they have come to occupy a fabled reality. To grasp it we must make an imaginative leap and put ourselves in the shoes of a person walking in a desert caravan.

For the desert traveler, a Bukhara, a Samarkand, was nothing more, or less, than an article of faith, a magic name you tied to the head of your mount, trusting that its syllables, sufficiently repeated, would somehow guide you through the surrounding inferno. For there was no way of ascertaining whether the city would be still there when and if you arrived. A Genghis Khan or a Timur might have happened by. The river along which it nestled might have shifted its banks. After several such shiftings, the city might have taken it into its head to move, oh, two hundred kilometers away, to a site where conditions seemed more stable.

One could imagine these legendary cities deflated by grim reality: the months on end of blistering heat and constantly swirling dust, the cacophony of a proletariat clanking around in all too audible chains. But the traveler, having survived so much, was little inclined to regard the city he had reached as anything but a much-vaunted paradise. The local merchants, dependent as they were on a continuing flow of goods brought by caravans, made sure that everything the traveler encountered catered to his illusion. Didn't the sign PARADISE greet him in the welcoming green of the city's gardens, the irrigated strand of unparalleled wealth that formed the first impression of the city? Once he was within the walls, it loomed again, transfigured into the shapes of celestial domes and minarets and an equally imposing array of madrasahs, or religious academies, their portals and courtyards shimmering in an Elysian field of tile.

One may see the traveler going from one miracle of blue to the next, eyeing in awe courtiers in their robes of filigreed silk and maybe even joining them in a bout of learned conversation. If distinguished enough, he might find himself summoned to a private audience with the reigning prince, to trade compliments that were virtual poems, where a less-than-perfect line could mean one's head.

If the city seemed a terrestrial paradise, it was, more tellingly, a stage set designed so that whoever possessed it could indulge himself in that greatest of roles, playing God. Hence the outsize scale of the architecture, reminding all who passed that they were, in theatrical perspective, specks of dust in the royal eye, chess pawns waiting to be played, puppets dangling on a string. Hence, too, the insistence on *style* in everything, from how you spoke to how you dressed. Such theater required specialized backstage personnel: artisans who did nothing but fashion dazzling watered-silk swords, or the equally renowned silk dyers, descendants of Jews borne into captivity by Nebuchadrezzar, readily distinguished by the purple dye on their hands.

As elsewhere, an art of illusion drew on a contrasting hyperrealism: perhaps a parade of bleating captives whose gouged eyes paid for a caravan raid carried out by their tribesmen; or the screams of an adulterous woman being spun in a burlap sack with a pair of wildcats. Theatrical dignity insisted that such public punishments be meted out in the great square adjoining the royal palace. A charlatan might swallow a sword or walk on water. But an emir outshone them by taking away life itself. And, as in all theater, performance was everything.

In time, the vogue spread until every petty despot wanted a civic theater of his own. There were khans whom nothing would satisfy until they could triumph on the boards of Samarkand itself. One has only to read Bābur's memoirs to realize how central to his self-image ruling Samarkand was. Only at the end of his life, after thirty years of incessant efforts—he captured the city several times, but never held it very long—did he allow himself to be consoled by the infinitely more tawdry prize of India.

———

As world civilizations go, the twenty-five-hundred-year-old Persian/Central Asian may not quite rank with the Indo-Chinese, let alone the European. But if, like Jefferson and Stendhal, you regard the pursuit of happiness as being up there with life and liberty as an inalienable human right; or if you are intrigued by a culture that addresses less the human than the angel in yourself, then Central Asia can seem a shining beacon. What better can a desert people aspire to than a city set, like a garden, in the here and now?

A garden need not be confined to any one *locus amoenus.* You could take it with you in the form of a carpet. Or it might glow over a city in the great dome of a mosque. It might even blazon forth in the calligraphed distichs of a ghazel. The idealism propelling it was basically Platonic. Only, in Central Asia, the world of essences that spilled and played in a riot of flowerlike colors, smells, bird calls, and water sounds was not the emanation of a distant cave-reflected "sun," but of your ruler: he whom you knelt before, whose smile gave your own its glow.

The culture was kept from elitist smugness by a keen awareness of the ravaging desert that lay outside the charmed enclosure. In this respect both the Hindu and the Persian are cultures firmly rooted in the moment. But where the Hindu moment can extend all the way back to the beginnings of existence, the man of the desert inevitably sees life as highly temporary and thus amoral. In Central Asia a man might not become transparent, but he could well become prismatic, and it was to that end these connoisseurs of sensation strove to refine sensibility.

In Central Asia we do not see enacted the dialectic of history as simple Marxism conceives it, where progressive and counter-progressive forces push one another against urban barricades. Instead, at the desert edge of one or another violently carved-out empire, history rather resembles a cyclone. And there is no way of anticipating from what quarter it will blow in next. At one moment, from the far reaches of the Black Sea, Alexander's Macedonian Greeks appear. They take to the prevailing theater as to the manor born, outfitting themselves in the most glamorous silks, staging a drunken brawl in which Alexander gets to kill his best friend while marrying a local Bukharan, Roxane.

A millennium later, out of the Arabian Desert, come the so-called People of the Book. Their occupation lasts little more than a century. But before they vanish, the fire and sword they believe in have triumphed over the long existing Zoroastrian-Nestorian legacy of good *and* evil, shadow *and* light.

Another four centuries, and the Scourges of God, as the Mongols call themselves, ride in on their little ponies from the other side of the Gobi Desert. The Scourges disapprove of theater. The great sets are razed and most of the backstage personnel are liquidated. The next century and a half is not a good time for theater.

Finally, out of all the dust and ashes, Central Asia launches a human cyclone of its own in the person of Timur, or Tamburlaine, as Christopher Marlowe called him. In the course of thirty-five helter-skelter years, Timur conquers everything from

Constantinople and Damascus to Delhi and Chinese Xinjiang. An amazingly rebuilt Samarkand finds itself the kingpin of what is now truly a world stage.

Timur's restorations may seem hasty, as one towering set after the next collapsed of its own weight even before it was finished. But the whirlwind Timur launched is such that his sons and grandsons—all the way to the sixth-generation Bābur—will go off looking for city theaters of their own: ones with better clay to build with, perhaps, or a more earthquake-resistant soil. They found such theaters in Herat, in the Isfahan of Shāh Abbās, in the changing capitals of Mogul India. It is what historians have been pleased to call the Timurid Renaissance.

———

For the Central Asian city-theaters straddling the Silk Road, Vasco da Gama's opening in 1498 of the sea route to India and China was little short of catastrophic. As the caravan cities declined, so did theater itself become increasingly kinky, not to say perverse. A troupe of painted dancing boys, a harem of Lolitas, who began at age eight or nine and were pensioned off once pregnant, was about all a nineteenth-century khan could delight and shock us with. As rumors got out and Western indignation rose, the emirs reacted huffily by declaring their cities off-limits. Any European venturing in would be treated as the spy he undoubtedly was and summarily executed.

Not surprisingly, few great gamesmen were willing to put their lives on the emir of Bukhara's line. The two who do famously blunder in, the British army officers Stoddart and Conolly, never seem to realize the rules of the game, let alone what is about to happen to them. Instead, they are convinced that their status as officers and envoys of Her Royal Majesty confers diplomatic immunity.

At first, the emir is gentle with them, confining them to the house of his fat artillery commander. There, he knows, they will be well fed, and some of their military expertise may rub off on their host. But when his beautifully penned letter to Her Majesty offering to conclude a treaty of alliance—it's a virtual poem from one epithet to the next—brings no reply other than an equivocal message from Lord Palmerston, he reacts as any un-read poet in his position would, by sentencing these two saints of the empire to his blackest dungeon. It may be he has failed to understand the difficulties besetting an understaffed bureau-cracy running an empire on which the sun never sets. Perhaps he believes in telepathy, in the sound of Stoddart's and Conolly's screams resonating where poetry has failed. At his wits' end, he even starts toying with their religious beliefs: "If you will con-vert to Islam . . ." Not meaning, of course, a word of it, but try-ing to break down the stolid wall of their psychic inhibitions. Fi-nally, realizing that he is becoming obsessed with theatrical gambits, he has them, in utter despair, executed.

By the standards of the day, the arrest of two British officers is so unbelievable that a man of the cloth, Joseph Wolff, takes it upon himself to journey all the way to Bukhara to ascertain what has befallen them. When the emir claps the reverend, too, in prison, he saves himself with a real act of theater—by playing the madman.

Forewarned is forearmed, and in 1863 the Hungarian Ar-minius Vambéry ventures by, disguised as a mendicant dervish from Constantinople. Vambéry was a gifted linguist, not only conversant with the major languages of Europe but also fluent in Persian, Turkish, and Arabic. The gripping account of his journey from the Caspian Sea across the terrifying Kara Kum Desert to Khiva, and then across the Kyzyl Kum Desert to Bukhara, is indispensable for anyone interested either in the slave-trading culture of Turkmenian nomads or in the theatrical reality of Central Asian city-states.

Reading Vambéry, it is hard to believe that the end is almost in sight, in the form of a Russian expeditionary force determined to close down such bloodcurdling anachronisms. In 1868, Bukhara falls. Five years later it is Khiva's turn. Is the slave mart pulled down and replaced with the present-day bazaar? Hardly. The clanking of chains and futile attempts at escape into the desert go on uninterrupted until 1917 and the Bolshevik coup d'état.

While capturing Khiva, one of the first commodities Russians notice is the fine Egyptian-type cotton farmed in Khwārizm for several millennia. Imagine the yields the coarser American variety might give! American cotton succeeds so well that Khwārizm is soon outproducing every province in Russia, a situation that still obtains. But to pick cotton by hand you need a cheap labor force—slaves, for example. This puts the Russians in a quandary, because Alexander II had emancipated the serfs in 1862. Forced to choose between their civilizing mission and their yen for cotton, the Russians decide that the conquest hasn't happened. Back onto his golden throne goes the khan as absolute master, and back into their shackles go the cotton pickers.

During the civil war between Whites and Reds, Samarkand sides with the Reds in order to be free of Bukhara. The victors reward Samarkand by making it the seat of the new dispensation. A ring of universities, medical facilities, and hospitals soon encircles the city. To irrigate the cotton fields, water is brought down from the mountains, in such quantities the climate is drastically altered. Skies that rarely saw a cloud are now overcast for much of the year. And the famous golden light—Samarkand is fifteen hundred miles from the nearest sea—becomes, too, a thing of the past.

While Samarkand prospered under Soviet rule, Bukhara and Khiva were left to wither and die. In the case of Bukhara, one of Islam's holiest cities, one understands the policy. The Soviets did not want to touch off a religious powder keg. They succeeded so well that, by 1932, when Ella Maillart visited Bukhara, a population of two hundred thousand had dwindled to a mere forty thousand hangers-on.

By the end of the Second World War, this deliberate neglect had come to look a bit like eating the goose that laid the golden egg. Today's Moscow has every reason to look like the impoverished, badly maintained Third World city that it is. The pre-1917 class structure of czar, boyars, bureaucrats, and serfs, with no intermediate commercial class, was not one geared to individual enterprise. But Bukhara, surviving at the edge of a great desert, has always been a city forced to live by its commercial and theatrical wits. Fortunately, an artisanal tradition survived and could be adapted to new industrial needs. In no time, a fairly elegant new Bukhara rose outside the old walls.

The collapse of the price of oil in the late seventies found the Soviet bureaucrats looking for sources of hard currency. It was inevitable they should recognize the potential drawing power of great Central Asian cities with magical names. What remained of the architectural heritage would be restored, and what had crumbled away would be re-created. One may feel these un-peopled "museums in the open" are little more than dressed-up ghost towns, but for most visitors, the restored sets are still capable of evoking a fabled reality. While waiting for a more open society—nothing less than full cultural autonomy will do—we can be grateful for the restoration that has saved something of these cities' extraordinary pasts.

———

Seeing the great cities of Central Asia has never been easy. Even now, in a time of perestroika, it's mostly package tourists who visit them. For some, it may not be undesirable to be shep-herded in a group from one official sight to the next. At least they go where so few Westerners have ever been, and they are not bankrupted in the process.

For the traveler who wants to linger a bit, getting there is more complicated, because the Intourist system is not geared to the needs of the private traveler. You have to be fitted into whatever accommodation hasn't been booked, and you have to spend the night, no matter what, in your Intourist hotel. Should you strike off on your own to visit an outlying shrine, you may find yourself on the next plane back to Moscow.

I had applied for a month's visa, listing Samarkand, Bukhara, and Khiva as the cities I wanted to visit. But I had neglected to discuss my plans with Intourist, assuming that the Writer's Union, which had invited me, was taking care of travel arrangements. I was told by the two delegates who met me at the airport—a new arrival was not allowed to wander about Moscow on his own—that I had narrowly escaped being put on the next flight back to London. Only at the last minute had a hotel room been found for me, across the river and a fifteen-minute bus ride from the Kremlin. There I would have to stay until my arrangements were in order.

This took another eight days. But the time was not entirely wasted. Some twenty years earlier I had traveled in Bulgaria, Hungary, and northern China, experiences I hadn't succeeded in getting down on paper, perhaps because I had allowed myself to be kept too far from people's lives. This time I was determined to refuse the invitations of taxis, the glamour of subways, and instead see what I could on foot. Such walking can be done, of course, but it leaves you, leaves everyone, exhausted. Those haggard faces, empty suitcases in hand, eyes riveted to the ground, testify to the difficulties of city life in the embattled North. But above all, they testify to the toll levied by the city's gargantuan scale, with its pitted, crumbling sidewalks, its half-mile-long blocks without benches, without shops, with nowhere to stop. After a while you just give up. Your mammoth hotel, with its warden, its restaurant on each floor, can begin to seem city enough.

Of the great Central Asian cities, Samarkand, two time zones southeast of Moscow, makes as pleasant a place to begin as any. Geographical situation has much to do with it, for it sits at the hub of a mountain-ringed natural crossroads, on a vast fertile oasis fed by two great rivers, the Amu Darya (the Oxus of classical antiquity), which was, for Arabs, one of the four rivers of paradise, and the Zeravshan, or "Strewer of Gold," where virtually anything grows. Elevation is also a factor: twenty-two hundred feet may not seem all that high, but it stands sixteen hundred feet higher than Bukhara, two hundred miles to the west, and the difference shows.

Like Rome, the city to which it is often compared, Samarkand has the advantages that come from being built on a series of hills. Wherever you turn your head, a minaret or dome is apt to pop up, glazed in a blue to rival the sky. And however hot it is—temperatures can range up to 120 degrees Fahrenheit—there is nearly always a breeze blowing; you have only to step into a bit of shade to feel a cooling dryness. Here, fifteen hundred miles from the nearest sea, swirling motes of dust take on a translucency that not only enables you to see unusually far but also gives to objects themselves—a man's beard, a woman's shawl, the arching entrance of a mosque—a soft, almost sculpted patina. At dawn, or in the afterglow of dusk, nothing is quite like it.

The fine-grained calcareous silt, or loess, constantly blown off the mountains gives the Samarkand valley its extraordinary fertility. Just about anything will grow in it. That for the past hundred years it has been mainly cotton, rather than melons or wine-making grapes, seems a pity, given the difficulties the

Soviet Union has in feeding its peoples. But cotton means big rubles, and it is hard to begrudge peasant collectives their evident prosperity.

If soil fertility has been the basis of Samarkand's prosperity, its strategic position at the fork of the Silk Road from China (one route leads south to Afghan Bactria and India, the other southwest to Herat and the Caspian Sea) has made it from time immemorial the Rome to which all traffic inevitably flowed. When Alexander's Macedonians appeared in 329 b.c., Samarkand was already a considerable city with an impregnable citadel and an outer rampart fourteen kilometers long circling it.

The region itself, which Kipling dubbed the "Back of Beyond," has gone by a number of names. To the Greeks and Romans it was Trans-Oxiana; to the Arabs, the Land between the Rivers; to the Elizabethans, Tartary. The celebrated fourteenth-century Moroccan traveler Ibn Battūtah knew it as Turkestan, a name it kept until 1930, when Stalin renamed it Uzbekistan after the Turkish-speaking, Mongol-featured Uzbek tribe that has dominated the countryside since 1550.

The original inhabitants were Persian-speaking, Indo-European people known as the Sogdians. Even today, despite a number of razings and the seemingly endless incursions of Turkish-speaking nomads, they still constitute a considerable proportion of the population of Samarkand and Bukhara. The enclave is large enough for there to be the beginnings of a nationalist movement (on the model of the Armenians of Nagorno-Karabakh) that aims to include the two cities in an expanded Tajikistan.

In appearance these Tajiks resemble the Persian-speaking Afghans of the Herat area. They lack the arching eyebrows, blue-black hair, and aquiline nose of typical Iranians, and are generally taller. The question as to how they have survived in this Central Asian melting pot is easily answered. Emerging from the bazaar, try sauntering down one of the old streets lined with ancient mulberry trees and two-story nineteenth-century houses. Likely as not, you will be confronted after a few paces by a man who politely tells you that you have wandered into a cul-de-sac. When the same thing keeps happening in every street, you begin to realize what an ancient people's notions of privacy may be about.

The Zoroastrian city that bewitched Alexander was known as Maracanda. When we next hear of it, after its conquest by the armies of the Arab caliphate under Kissam-ibn-Abbas, it is called Afrasiab. In 1220, Genghis Khan appears, and the hill of Afrasiab becomes what it remains to this day, a gigantic cemetery. Sa, possibly from Sart, the name the Persian-speaking town dwellers called themselves until 1917, is placed before Maracanda, and we have Samarkand.

That most silken of names was almost enough. All that remained was for a visionary to come along who would turn it into the Rome of Central Asia. The visionary was Timur (1336? to 1405), otherwise known as Tamerlane, the greatest conqueror the world has ever known.

Timur belongs to a recognizable type, the self-made sports-loving businessman who has come up through the ranks. Only in Timur's time, the major business was war. Historians tell us that continual war of the kind Timur waged inevitably ends by draining a nation of its lifeblood and bankrupting it. Under Timur, however, war unquestionably paid for itself. His campaigns were organized as systematic lootings, hostile takeovers, each territorial acquisition bankrolling the next.

We usually think of our chieftains as fighting for some ideal—human rights, God's glory, peace and prosperity, a war to end all wars, a nation's way of life. But Timur's sole purpose in fighting was more crude: to keep going, to stay in the field. To the art of war he brought as single-minded a concentration as we have ever known. We blanch at the ruthlessness of a leader who can order the slaughter of the male population of any city foolish enough to resist him. But that was the name of the game—kill or be killed—and, after thirty-five years of Timur, you would think his foes might have had an idea of the odds, of what awaited them were their gamble to fail.

The Timur who never lifted a siege was hardly likely to grow impatient after a month's resistance and march off after easier prey. With his reputation constantly on the line, he did exactly what circumstances required. The same governing rationality extended to former rulers, whom he maintained as regents, and the lenient taxation he favored. Unlike so many Central Asian despots, Timur was not vain or wantonly cruel. He always served a principle, something larger.

I find it hard not to admire a chieftain who, before proceeding into battle, would have his officers listen to the recital of a defeat suffered as a result of self-satisfaction and insufficient preparation by one of his forebears. In an underling the one failing he would not countenance was being lied to.

A Turkish speaker of part-Mongol extraction, Timur hailed not from Samarkand, but Shahr-i-Sabz, a pretty town forty miles and a couple of mountain passes away. As a young warrior he seems to have conceived a passion for the big city akin to what one of us might entertain for our local ball team. When he seized Samarkand, it was, as a major city, respectable enough— up there in third or fourth place behind Urganch and Bukhara in the Central Asian League.

Most owners would have been satisfied with that; you can't buck tradition. But the fan in Timur wanted Samarkand on top of not only the Central Asian League but the All-Asian League as well. The object of his campaigns remained the acquisition of new taxable domains and all the loot he and his men could stagger away with. No matter how far afield campaigns took him, he never stopped thinking about, and recruiting for, Team Samarkand: architects, masons, tile layers, and even the odd musician or intellectual for his own court. Looking at all he built, I can't help but feel that advancing Samarkand to its rightful spot as premier garden city preceded any notion of the place he would occupy in the *World Conquerors Record Book*. It was only late in his career, after Samarkand's first-place position was assured (only China remained to be conquered), that he began to think seriously of the benefits of a world under a single authority. "As there is one Allah in heaven," he argued, not implausibly, "so should there be but a single viceroy on earth." By then, that's what he virtually was, Mr. World Government.

There is a well-known story of Timur, while in Shiraz, summoning the great Persian poet, Hāfez, to an audience. The poet, an old man by then, appeared before Timur dressed in tatters. Timur reminded Hāfez of the poem in which he says he would give all of Bukhara's "vaunted gold, and all the gems of Samarkand," for one last sight of his beloved.

"How dare you," Timur asked, "give away what's not yours, but mine?"

Without missing a beat, Hāfez replied, pointing to his rags, "You can see where such prodigality has gotten me."

Timur's prodigality went into building. For most anyone else, Samarkand's position on the Silk Road would have sufficed. One had only to wait and merchants would arrive. But Timur understood *l'homme moyen sensuel,* who might travel as much for pleasure and edification as for profit. To obtain goods in sufficient quantities, he had to entice travelers, and with what better than a show of stupendous domes? As one marvel succeeded another, one can imagine world curiosity mounting: what will Timur amaze us with next?

When the Spanish envoy, Ruy González de Clavijo, appeared in 1404, Timur's oeuvre was basically complete. A deep moat girded the city. In turn, the moat was protected by a many-towered crenellated wall. The wall's ramparts were, in most places, wide enough for a rider to gallop along. From the central hub, the Registan, broad thoroughfares radiated out to six gates. Outside the walled city, thirteen different parks waited, with fountains, plunging terraces, summer palaces, and pavilions. In a mere twenty days, Clavijo witnessed the demolition and construction of an enormous bazaar that extended from the Bibi Khanum Mosque all the way to the Amu Darya River. Fountains lined the central axis, which sported a series of cupolas where shoppers could shelter from the sun. The trades, too, had their own bazaars, some more distinguished than others. In papermaking and the production of crimson damask, the city, according to Bābur, had no equal.

Since the buildings were made of nothing but loess dust faced with mud, it is remarkable that anything should be left standing. Nonetheless, a trio of structures have survived: the Shah-e-Zindeh Necropolis complex; the very large Bibi Khanum Mosque; and the Gur Emir Mausoleum, in which Timur lies buried. Together, they offer a testament to Timur and his vision.

Of the three, the Shah-e-Zindeh, or "Living King" (built between 1360 and 1415 on the site of an earlier complex on the southern slope of the ruined city of Afrasiab), is aesthetically the most rewarding. It commemorates the spot where Kissam-ibn-Abbas, a cousin of the Prophet Muhammad and the founder of Islam in Central Asia, hemmed in by pursuers, found the earth beneath him opening in the form of a well, into which he disappeared—the well, obviously, of the living faith from which Central Asians drink to this day. One can see it suiting the magus in Timur to have Kissam's well spouting forth a wealth of blue tile.

In honoring the local saint, Timur hoped to placate the devout who may have felt, as the Imam of the Ismail-e-Bokhari Shrine said in regard to Iran's Khomeini, that "all this incessant warfare isn't very Muslim." But he had the pathway leading to Kissam's shrine lined with a series of personal mausoleums—a beloved aunt here, a family guru there. The complex must have been planned as a bridge linking the founder of one enterprise with that of another.

From afar, the Shah-e-Zindeh's domes call out, their robin's-egg blue beckoning past the yellow browns of the surrounding city. Once through the mosque's archway, you gain the complex by way of an unusually wide, twenty-six-step stairway. At the top, in an elevation as much spiritual as physical, you find yourself in a little village of sorts. On each side of the sunken walkway leading to Kissam's tomb lie the dead Timur has chosen to honor. Each has his set of rooms, but the interiors, for all their stalactite-dripping corner vaulting and ribbed five-pointed domes, are overshadowed by the outer facade's fanfare of color. By now you have forgotten about the domes, which in any case you can no longer see. Instead you are swept along in a blaze of tile. Vertically alternating strips of blue, or blue and white—rather like the borders of a carpet—contrast with a silhouette-carved high relief, in which turquoise flowers jut forth from a darker lapis lazuli background. And above, from another archway, more tile flowers peer, birdlike.

Invented a century earlier in Andalusia, majolica had just reached Central Asia. As you proceed, you can't help but notice the advance in technique. In twelve years, the flanking panels widen, allowing a new, more resonant blue to sing out against explosions of orange, green, and black. Tribal restraint has given way to joyful color for color's sake. Even the gold inscriptions become a dance in themselves, of cursive writing threaded through flowers. And new colors keep being found. Here, for instance, a facade features tiny red-centered flowers set in a wealth of green. Yet it's the yellow that, for good or bad, stands out, catches the eye with its novelty.

Compared to Timur's later buildings, the Shah-e-Zindeh is unpretentious. Yet in the joy of its carving, all those blue-purple notes bouncing against our eyes, it is, as Joseph Brodsky notes, like coming upon a shoal of "corals in the desert." You can feel as if you have stepped into the intimate soul of an empire.

———

The Bibi Khanum Mosque (1399 to 1404) reveals Timur in a more Cecil B. DeMille mood. From his successful Indian campaign he has returned with ninety-seven teams of elephants. For what, other than warfare, can they be used? Immediately the notion of a mosque, bigger and more ornate than anything in his conquered realms, springs to mind. Dedicating it to his senior consort, the emperor of China's daughter, he has it built next to the new bazaar, sustaining a fertile connection that has long accompanied the spread of Islam.

Descriptions have come down of the old man personally overseeing the construction and, from his place on the scaffold, tossing coins and scraps of meat to the workers below. As can be imagined, the work progressed at an unheard-of pace. From the marble quarries forty kilometers away, 480 stone pillars were cut and transported to Samarkand by elephant. In three months, the minarets were erected. During one of his inspections, Timur noticed that the adjoining bazaar was not spacious enough. Up went the new fountain-lined bazaar Clavijo described. Returning from still another campaign, he noticed the central portal lacked authority and set a more imposing one in its place.

The great vault of the mosque's central dome may not, as one poet put it, have rivaled heaven itself, nor could the central portal have outshone the Milky Way, but the Bibi Khanum was certainly very large. (Its modern replica is about a third smaller.)

One gold inscription, Bābur reports, could be read a mile away. The three inner rooms were of such a size that, to keep the walls from buckling on the spot, all the in-between niches had to be filled and replaced with buttresses. Even before the mosque was consecrated, the bricks and much of the plaster had begun to flake from the dome. In no time at all, the minarets, the stone columns holding up the cupola galleries, and the vaults of the outer domes and portals had all collapsed.

In explanation, the story is told how the mosque's Persian architect, as his price for finishing before Timur's return, insisted on a kiss from Bibi Khanum herself. She, of course, refused. But when word reached her that Timur was in Merv, a week's march away, and the mosque was still unfinished, she decided to allow the architect to kiss her cheek through her veil. Unfortunately, the Persian's kiss burned such a hole that a black spot appeared on her skin. To conceal it, the princess attired herself and her entire court in veils. When Timur learned what had happened, he had her burned at the stake. As Timur's men were pursuing the architect up the scaffolding to the top of the dome, wings suddenly sprouted on his shoulders, and off he flew to the holy city of Mashhad in northwest Iran, the next site, appropriately, of Timurid architecture.

Some buildings may look better as ruins; photographs of the Bibi Khanum taken before the 1975 restoration show the badly cracked and utterly romantic dome in much deeper original blues. But the project of rebuilding a structure on Bibi Khanum's titanic scale could not help but appeal to the Kremlin. And, despite local protests—"This isn't restoration, it's wholesale invention"—her elephantine structure has contributed a new blue of its own to the Samarkand skyline.

When soon thereafter Timur commissioned the Gur Emir Mausoleum, nominally to commemorate a favorite grandson and former heir apparent, his taste had changed. Nothing less than the costliest minerals would do. The waist-high inside wall panel is a warm, yellow-green onyx. A pierced alabaster railing guards the tomb site. The great slab adorning Timur's own grave is a single chunk of nephrite jade excavated and somehow brought back intact from Hotan in western China. There was even a white circular rug, still visible seventy years ago, in which an arabesque and flower design, woven into a perfectly matched white background, contained space in the middle for a malachite-veined tombstone.

Such ostentation usually affronts. But the Gur Emir carries it off. With its flower-tiled walls, its airy lavender-and-gold ceiling beaming down like the eye of an enormous sunflower, the mausoleum is all of a piece. In the surrounding effects, in Timur's chiseled admonition, "If I were still alive, humanity would not be glad," in the entombed mullah at whose feet he has placed himself, we feel the presence of a man who knows himself and feels no regret.

The good fortune that allowed Timur to fight to a ripe age served him even in death. Other graves are robbed, but when the eighteenth-century Persian conqueror Nāder Shāh tries to prize loose Timur's nephrite jade slab, he is obliged to desist after cracking it in two. The Soviets are less superstitious. They want to honor Timur with a life-size statue and, to get the dimensions right, they haul him on June 21, 1941, out of his grave to confirm that he was, at five feet eight inches, above average height for a Tatar, red-bearded, and lame in his right arm and leg. It's no accident, the locals believe, that this was the very day Adolf Hitler invaded the Soviet Union.

In Samarkand, Timur's successor was his grandson, Ulūgh Beg, the only son of Shāh Rokh and Robert Byron's heroine, Gohar

Shad. Ulūgh Beg was one of the world's great astronomers. His calculations of the earth's calendar, made from the data his impressive observatory had collected, were a mere six hours off. His dream, as ruler, was to make Samarkand the center of a new enlightenment. To attract intellectuals, he built at the central Registan an academy intended to outshine anything extant in Central Asia. Where another's investment in plant might have included a gymnasium or a great library, Ulūgh Beg went in for tile, acres and acres of blue shimmering wall. The effect was such that his successors built two more academies in even fancier tile. What one feels about this grandiose architecture, without the street life that made the Registan teem like a second San Marco, is a matter of opinion. But it is indisputable that this naturally echoing space, with its vast open portals and recessed arches, does make quite a concert hall.

It has been argued that the Timurid dynasty's real artistic achievements are to be found not in Samarkand, but in the great buildings Gohar Shad would erect in Herat and Mashhad, in the Herat school of miniature painting, and in the Mogul art of northern India. But theater, on this kind of civic scale, makes for a rather impure art form. We judge it by its impact, the energy waves it sends out, its ability to keep us sitting, enthralled, night after night, year after year. That Timur's theater could go on playing for the next couple of centuries in Bukhara, and four hundred years later was still running strong in Khiva, speaks volumes for the energy he set in motion.

Everyone I met in Samarkand kept mentioning the Soviet invasion of Afghanistan and wringing their hands. But could not the same be said about the mid-nineteenth-century Russian annexation of Turkestan? The Russians have just celebrated their millennium as a Christian nation. Samarkand celebrated its twenty-five-hundred-year civic anniversary in 1970. And it must be said that having to cope, over all this time, with the whims of Greeks, Arabs, Persians, Mongols, and Uzbeks has made for a people well adapted to the exigencies of modern life.

In Moscow, the disruption caused by the 1917 revolution was such that, even today, very little works. The nearest shopping center is, as they say, seven thousand miles away. But in Samarkand, things work. One can see why vacationing Russians prefer it to the resorts of Crimea. I can't imagine a better city in which to pursue a tan.

These realizations took a while to sink in. My first days were largely spent sightseeing and taking excursions. There may not be too much wrong with gadding about, for an oasis, after all, includes its surroundings. And I needed time to hone my eyes before I could think of sitting somewhere and letting a bazaar's faces, caps, moustaches, and costumes speak to me.

———

As I sit on a teahouse's terrace overlooking the market, I find myself absorbing a new tempo. *Ever slower* might well define it. The steepness of the city's hills, the fierceness of the noon sun take their toll. Unless I can feel a breeze, I don't stir. Better to re-hydrate with a pot of green tea or duck into the cool of a bathhouse. By the time I emerge, chances are a breeze will have sprung up, a beneficence irrigating me as I stroll.

For confirmation, observe the motorized traffic. In other cities we know how it proceeds: honking, swearing, shaking its dread fists. In Samarkand, not a car, or even a motorcycle, would think of advancing at anything above a crawl. The streets, they are aware, do not belong to them.

In olden days, domestic life went on behind blue-painted compound doorways, in the secluded fastness of a courtyard. Nowadays, the courtyards are deserted. All you find is the family car and lines of drying laundry. Domestic life has moved onto the streets. It is there you find people of an evening, propped on a bench against the wall or squatting on their heels in a barbed-wire-enclosed weed patch, casually observing the passersby, the whirligigs of children's games.

This may sound as if city life were a matter of *dolce far niente*. On the contrary, people work hard, and Uzbekistan outranks any Soviet province in productivity. But for the Sart, work is only a means to an end, which is abundance. He wants to be surrounded by 12.3 children, by his own admirable girth. He would not dream of going anywhere without stopping off on the way to nibble something, a cone of sunflower seeds, a packet of pistachio nuts, a pastel sherbet. The plates presented in an eatery are modest in size, but every inch is piled in little towers. There is nothing distanced, finicky, in greetings. The whole face, at the sight of a friend, lights up. The look is returned, just as vividly. Then the two embrace, clasping each other by the shoulders.

The notion of twelve children in the average family would have most of us throwing up our hands. A surer recipe for poverty and ecological disaster is hard to imagine. But in a well-educated community, large families can make for vigorous dynamism. Workers compete with one another and, as in Japan, numbers may allow you to plan. In a time of shifting values, numerous children may offer needed insulation. It's not, Sarts claim, large families that take up one's time, but middle-sized ones. Large families run themselves. And parents, in staking out a compound, make sure there is room for children to add houses of their own. A Russian will happily move for the sake of a better job. To a Sart it's unthinkable.

Life in Samarkand has been organized on the same totalitarian model as in Moscow: blockbuster hotels like the one I have to stay in and thirty-thousand-person collective farms. If it works somewhat better in Samarkand, it is because of the meticulousness of the planning. Extra labor is never trucked in to help with the harvest; despite the lack of machines, the work gets done. This may be because the supervisor and his staff are always meeting. You see them gathering after dinner to plan to the last man-hour the next day's deployment. In my hotel, courses actually appear, one after another. Within minutes, the dining area will metamorphose from a theater to a restaurant to a nightclub's roaring, vodka-besotted, ocean-liner-style dance hall.

But central planning invites local corruption. As I arrived, a trial was under way of several party officials who had invented for themselves a vast acreage of cotton fields, bilking the nation of some three billion rubles. I was shown stocks of lethal chemicals that had been showered on collective farms before their effects had been researched. The wine production that might bring in foreign currency fell victim to a zealously interpreted antialcohol campaign. Rather than uproot his twenty-five-hundred-year-old grapes, one manager of a Georgian collective chose to take his own life—an event that shocked even Moscow.

A Russian friend maintains you can tell a country's soul by its poetry. For those of us ignorant of local language, music does almost as well. In my case, nothing equals what I can learn from the dance music of a wedding. The trick, of course, is finding it. But once you have barged in, everything is taken care of. The father of the bride may be loath to wine and dine another neighbor, but an outsider's gaping mouth and amazed, beaming eyes can evoke unsuspected hospitality. In Moscow, I had met students who had managed to feed themselves, while in Samarkand, by going from one wedding to the next for months on end.

With their large families, you might think marriages occur

every day. But May does not have the fruits, the bursting melons, of September and October. I wasn't up to hanging out by the central Lenin memorial to wait for wreath-layers to come by fresh from the registry office. As for proudly braying cars, they always disappeared before I could ascertain where they were headed.

Finally I was down to my last night. Not only was it a Saturday, but also it was the eve of the monthlong Muslim fast of Ramadan. If music were to be found, it would be this evening. In that hope I struck out through the warren of lanes directly behind the Gur Emir Mausoleum.

I had walked for some time when I came to a house with a festive carpet slung over the street wall and a group of men lined up on chairs outside the main portal. Inside a doorway across the street women milled about, while both sides of the street had little tables piled with cakes and sweets. It seemed to be exactly what I was looking for.

I walked on. At the corner of the house, just out of sight, I came upon another group of young men, whose invitation to sit down I willingly accepted. In lovely twilight, it was a pleasure to sit with people who weren't afraid of Big Brother and who might actually talk to me. They had a teapot making its rounds, did I want some? I certainly did, and in a little while a teapot of my very own arrived, along with a plate of almond cookies and turnovers. The sweets were stacked one on top of the other, with a generosity that never ceased to impress. In no time, another dish, of meat dumplings, was brought. With me in one chair and my food on another, my hosts took the opportunity to rearrange themselves, two to a chair. Was it a wedding? I asked in sign language. No, I learned, it was the party after a funeral.

The sight of platters being spirited around the wall attracted the principal mourner, a handsome, self-confident professor of cybernetics in Samarkand University's mathematics department.

It was his father, he related in excellent English, a high court judge in Tashkent, who had died at the age of sixty-four.

Before we could talk further, he was called away to greet an arrival, leaving the rest of us to struggle on as best we could. For my part, I possessed several dozen words of Persian, learned half a lifetime ago. Two of them had a smidgen of English learned at school, the rest mere names plucked from newspapers. Yet, for the better part of two hours we carried on, pulling out various loaves and fishes: Gorbachev, Reagan, perestroika, Muhammad Ali, Angela Davis, Platini, Wilt Chamberlain. Finally, all our vocabulary milked, I rose to my feet, to discernible relief. They had met a real challenge; but from their faces I could tell how hard such hospitality had been.

Night had fallen when I started back to my hotel. I hadn't gone more than a few blocks when I picked up the strains of a wedding band. In the middle of a lane cordoned off by a length of green plastic, a clarinet and accordion played before several long tables of diners. The music was the enchantment I knew from my time in Greece, sprightly handkerchief-twirling *karsilimas,* bouncy shoulder-wiggling two-steps of the "Doctor, Doctor" persuasion. But, instead of linking bubbles together in a running medley, the musicians stopped after each dance, which did not give me the momentum needed to crash through to a table. This finally allowed me to tear myself away. The evening had, I realized, already happened. I wanted to walk back while I still retained my impressions: the look of the skullcaps; the arched eyebrows squeezed onto half of a chair; all that magical, one-rabbit-after-the-next hospitality plucked out of golden air.

BUKHARA

The city of Bukhara lies four hundred kilometers to the west of Samarkand and five hundred meters lower. Nearing it, the Zeravshan River, by now little more than a trickle, throws up its hands and dives into the earth, never to reappear. Ten kilometers to the other side of the city, the infamous Kyzyl Kum Desert begins. It stretches as far as Khwārizm, a crossing of two nights and a day by train. Where Samarkand's soil is a fertile yellow-brown loess, Bukhara's is an alkaline gray so drenched in accumulated salt that only ten percent is arable. To grow anything, you have to irrigate. But irrigation is no panacea, as the salt it brings has to be gotten rid of. Before planting cotton, a crop even more dominant than around Samarkand, the fields must be repeatedly washed—anywhere from two to twenty times. They are then attacked with weed killer. Add the defoliants that must be used if cotton is to be picked by machine and you grasp why the only place birds occur in any number is at the edge of the desert. The great symbol of Bukhara, the stork—their nests once bulged from the top of every minaret—hasn't been seen since 1974.

Unlike Samarkand, Bukhara is not set on a great caravan crossroads. To survive, it has had to rely on its hands and brains. In the Middle Ages its reputation for learning drew students from all over the Muslim world. "Elsewhere in the world," Fitzroy Maclean relates, "light came down from heaven; but from Bukhara it went up." It may be this intellectual tradition which helped persuade the Uzbeks, when they came to power, to make Bukhara instead of Samarkand the regional capital, a position it held until 1917. The region, which extends to the Afghan border, gave its name to the famous carpets.

Of the architectural heritage much survives. Bukhara's soil may not be as fertile as Samarkand's, but buildings stay up in it and some twenty are genuine masterpieces, ranging from the exquisite ninth-century Samanid Mausoleum to the prerevolutionary Summer Palace.

Within the array of monuments is the living expanse of the

mud-walled town, hardly changed in the last four hundred years. The windowless, thick-walled houses may lack most modern amenities, but they are well insulated, and any inconvenience may be preferable to the terror of living suspended in an earthquake-prone apartment block.

Upon finding yourself thrust into the old town's seething labyrinth, your immediate reaction may well be one of intense elation. The journey, at last, has snapped into focus.

In piecing together a picture of Samarkand, I had to allow for present conditions: distortions of weather, light, polluted skies, invented restorations, and all the rest. Even then I was perforce making do with fragments. In Bukhara, under a sky of a blue such as I had never beheld, and against a resonant mud-walled background, caps, turbans, dresses, robes flashed with a sharpness miraculously intact. I had moved into another world, almost another age.

But before I could start putting names to the novelties I was seeing, I had to get my bearings. And this, for all the unusually wide streets, could not have been more infuriating. I had given myself a reasonably visible destination, the great Tower of Death. Twenty-five minutes' walk away, its phallic beacon rose above the ancient end of the city skyline. Between me and it, the city fathers had placed four identical bazaars. With their overlapping turtle-shell domes—perfect jungle gyms for the kids!—the round bazaars were justly renowned seventeenth-century additions. But as pedestrian rotaries, with their gates striking off on every angle but the axis I was traversing, they amplified confusion. By the second or third bazaar I was back where I had started.

A similar feeling of blind man's bluff may hold for anyone confronted with Central Asian ornamentation. If there is a perspective ordering the labyrinth of gestures, it is certainly a different one from the standing, eye-level perspective that Giotto,

Uccello, and company developed. But how this difference makes its effect is difficult to understand.

One evening, as I was watching a wedding party dance, it struck me that the hand gestures I was taking in resembled the ornamentation on the carved doors I had puzzled over all afternoon.

Throughout Islam, one comes upon depictions of a privileged state of being: a pool, a garden, a place of joy. For us of the West (as for the Buddhists), desire can't help but be an illusion. But for the Muslim, desire amounts to nothing less than who you can will yourself to be—a self united with God. If so, every shrine must tell us how we too can reach that ecstatic self-realization.

How, viewing a room or the dome of a mosque, are we to place ourselves? No, not upright on a chair. Not squatting, effortlessly balanced, on our heels either. Instead I find myself sprawled in a corner of the floor, on back and elbows like a tea drinker in a yurt.

As I sprawl, what captures my eye is the point farthest away, infinity itself pouring many-splendored fireworks from its starry sky. Yes, God has many names. And it is the height from which it comes, and the sum of the ornamentation leading the eye up to such inclusive splendor, that gives a dome religious power. This may be why in Islamic art the perspective is not the eye-level horizontal version familiar to us. Instead, ornamentation hangs above us in a Tiepolo-like space, but we are not, as in a Tiepolo palace, lying in a four-poster looking up at it, those rosy nymphs and sporting satyrs; instead, we are sprawled in the unseemly dust.

Sprawled there, the possibility of perspective occurs. If there is an ecstatic source from which a dome's wealth of ornament radiates toward the beholder, should not the ornamentation visually intensify as it ascends? Look at the brickwork patterns of a minaret, how they intensify at the point where galleries break out and come into flower. Notice how, in a drawing room, the ornamentation goes berserk as the eye approaches upper corners: hanging stalactite grottos, magnificently orchestrated geometric fountains, dizzying color glowing between ceiling beams, one glorious riff after the next carved in Allah's name. Or notice the reliefs on walls, where flat surfaces have been set vibrating with a mesmerizing variety of perforations, niches, alcoves, and mirrored recesses.

The amount of labor such a vision requires may seem prohibitive. How does a house ever get finished? But what's wrong with a single superlatively intricate student room? Even in the most elegant palaces, beautifully worked rooms and utter dilapidation can lie within a few feet of one another without anyone feeling the least embarrassed.

As to the impulses that fueled the ornamentation, one can only speculate. Henri Michaux maintains there is no provision in the Koran for labyrinthine architecture and suggests opium or marijuana. Then again, it may be shortsighted to expect a billiard-ball causality to pop out of the Koran. The same phenomenon, Michael Beard argues, could be just as well explained by juxtaposing the forms Islam inherited from Byzantine architecture with the bouncy, antinarrative quality of the Koran.

———————

Cultural historians are wont to talk as if art forms progress and mature as their practitioners develop them. I am struck, on the contrary, by how often the work that announces a new direction remains unsurpassed. What holds for Homer, or for the novels of Cervantes, Fielding, Laclos, and Stendhal, holds equally for the architectural jewel that is Bukhara's Samanid Mausoleum. Built by the Persian-speaking ruler Esmāīl and completed before 907, it marks not only the first use of baked bricks in Central Asia but also the first mausoleum. It ranks, with Isfahan's twelfth-century Friday Mosque, as one of the most beautiful brick buildings ever built.

The mausoleum measures a scant thirty-one feet on each side. But the slightly swollen adobe base on which it stands and the way the corner columns lean in, narrowing as they rise, create a presence almost monumental. The effect, when combined with the rhythms of the brick, the jutting knobs, the perforated wheels, diamonds, and honeycombs, is of an intensively layered, percussive symphony. It reverberates out on every side, in every timbre of voice, and the more you walk around it, the more aware you become of the rhythmic clapping, the shouting out in joy, of a whole, singularly patterned work of art. Because of the clays used in the dome, the mausoleum changes with each hour of the day, becoming, as commentators agree, most vibrant of all at night.

Even today people place votive candles in the holes and niches, while questions and poems written on scraps of paper are carried into the tomb to be illuminated. The same feelings of affection may have inspired the Bukhariots to bury the mosque rather than see it razed by Genghis Khan's invading horde. There it remained until a Bolshevik soldier happened to poke its mound with a pitchfork. Perhaps only in the world of the *Arabian Nights* could one of the world's great buildings vanish into a seven-hundred-year hole in the ground. But from that deep slumber it has emerged, so very youthful and mysterious.

The heart of Bukhara, from the twelfth century on, has been the Kalyan Minar, or Tower of Death. One would expect a slender, tapering 164-foot-high building to have collapsed long ago. But minarets, by virtue of conical design, ride out seismic shocks better than most structures, and the Tower of Death was built to last. To ensure that the composition of sand and clay out of which the bricks were cast would be resistant enough, the construction overseer had ten coins buried in each pile. The piles were then pounded down until the last coin was flattened. When the bricks were finally formed and sunbaked, they were laid out in a long row and the overseer galloped his horse over them. If any splintered, the lot was redone. More recently, a rock climber gave it his own going over. The tower may not be Everest, but it must have made an impressive ascent.

A stone's throw from the Tower of Death lie the infamous royal dungeons. Why Westerners fail to visit them is hard to say, but at any hour of the day one comes upon busloads of Soviet tourists peering into well-like depths. Here and there a wall has been cut away; in the resulting gloom one takes in lifelike exhibits of prisoners bent over or listlessly crawling about, chained by a variety of shackles: manacles, ankle chains, neck collars linked to pegs by twenty-foot chains. The oubliettes were so deep the prisoners had to be lowered in by rope. There they lingered, sharing flung scraps of food with their fellow inmates and surviving the attentions of specially bred, three-inch-long tarantulas, until such time as the emir "should deign to remember them."

———

By 1900, Bukhara boasted a wealth of mosques, everything from the outlying Namazgah, big enough to accommodate the whole oasis (and used but twice a year), to the tiny, four-turreted Chor Minor (1807), built for nothing more than a library and a pair of storks. With what, the emir asks, can I amaze God? A children's mosque, why not? He knows of a folk craftsman, Shirin Muradov, who wants to build the emir an art nouveau summer palace five miles out of town. Why not test him with the Bala Hauz Mosque, an eighteenth-century eyesore a bowshot from the castle, and see what he can do to enliven it?

One expects a children's mosque to be small. The Bala Hauz, however, involves a two-page spread of a colonnaded porch facing out on a reflecting pool, so high ceilinged that it utterly conceals the mosque itself. Paint has just made its appearance in Central Asia. Where does it go? Up on the ceiling, naturally, applied in carpetlike strips between great beams, and in what can only be described as bursts of melting fireworks over the three frontal arches. Supporting the bedazzlement of dripping color are two rows of columns tapered to look like royal palm trees. You might almost be in a Buddhist *gompa,* such is the feeling of freedom and childlike delicacy that radiates from the blazes of pattern.

Muradov's Summer Palace, the so-called Museum of Regional Design, is a more equivocal achievement. The grounds, with peacocks, chukars, and a variety of Asian pheasants calling out from their Soviet-installed cages, can make you think you have lit upon nothing more than a raucous avian zoo. But inside the palace peacocks appear again, only now the tails with their dazzling eyes fan upward, ever broader, the entire length of a tiled wall.

As your eyes take you, clapping and cheering, from one triumph of kitsch to the next, you can't help but feel this is the magician's palace to end all palaces. An enormous white-on-white silhouette-carved reception hall leads into a room where the magic is all of glass; colors extend from the great windows' eerie tints of crimson and algae green all the way to a mirrored ceiling. Even this is surpassed by the art nouveau–inspired banquet hall: surely, one of the true wonders of the world, you mutter to yourself, awed by the vastness of a yellow ceiling whose gilt-striped columns bear the image of a three-eyed frog (green, blue, and brown and white) framed in a pink-and-blue arch. A yellow panel drops onto a glass-surrounded crown of lilac overlooking a tall, crimson, and diamond-inlaid chest of drawers. Decked out with a gold-plated service for fourteen, and with a peacock-clad footman posted behind each chair to pass the water pipes, dining there must have been delightful.

After the meal, guests retired to a pavilion across the garden. If a guest could tear himself away from the distractions of stalactite ceilings, of niched walls with peekaboo libraries, he might nap in a flower-tiled alcove, under a crown of stars and starflowers winking encouragingly from the vaulted milk-white ceiling.

Muradov's melding of art nouveau and Central Asian design is not architecture that travels well. One feels almost grateful for a revolution that prevented further excesses. All the same, wandering from one raucous-voiced example of courage to the next, it's hard not to feel something of the excitement presented by a bird-bright tropical forest. This is giddy stuff.

The old town of Bukhara grew up around the royal citadel and the Tower of Death in what is today the southwest part of the modern city. By the seventeenth century, the population had grown so that a new town center, the Liabi Hauz, or pool, had to be built outside the walls. The pool in question forms a large square framed by giant four-hundred-year-old mulberry trees. On one side, a series of steps—the tiny lips of *liabi?*—rises to the water-reflected arch of the Nadir Divan-bigi khanaqah. Across from this Sufi center, set a hundred yards back from the pool, is a religious academy, its great portal faced with a tile relief depicting a pair of dragon peacocks flying toward each other as if to embrace. A small park, with trees, benches, and a sherbet stall, leads from the academy to the poolside restaurants, where bed tables, steps, and overhanging balconies are all painted the same creamy turquoise. The whole scene, replete with charcoal smells of outdoor cooking, three geese scrounging at your feet, men in their various mufti lounging on the bed tables, and ancient music wailing down through the trees—each sob like the curve of an arch—could not be more like the *Arabian Nights*.

After securing a seat, diners line up in front of one of three outdoor kitchens. The first provides stew, the second marinated chicken, and the third, spicy dumplings along with the national rice dish, *pelao*. The *pelao* is served from an enormous conical trough. Taking an aluminum cooking pot in hand—it is what your serving will be weighed in—the cook scrapes some carrots from the bottom of the trough and ladles in a chunk or two of lamb topped by a big helping of rice. A dollop of pomegranate juice, a sprinkle of scallions and possibly raisins, and it is weighed on the scale—in Central Asia you always pay for quantity—and served with a thick slice of bread.

A *pelao*'s quality comes from the lamb fat in which it is cooked. The so-called tail that produces the fat is actually part of the back that projects over the legs and sways with every movement of the lamb's body. It is instructive to watch the women in a market going from one 150-pound animal to the next, their practiced fingers pinching a tail or removing a bit from the rear and sniffing it, tasting it. Fat is, to a Sart, what olive oil is to a Mediterranean or butter to a Norman. Everything is cooked in it. My Russian interpreter disapproved of the practice. So much grease could not be good for you. But in a dry climate, your skin may need a certain intake of fat to keep from withering up.

Central Asians find sheep without these tails incomprehensible. One turn-of-the-century traveler tells of a Sart exclaiming at the sight of sheep hanging in a Parisian butcher stall, "Why, they're dogs!"

Once the diner deposits the *pelao* at his table, he joins two further queues: one, for some tastier bread, across the square; another for a pot of tea. In bygone days there might have been a considerable choice of different teas; merchants prided themselves on being able to tell variety by mere touch. Nowadays the only variety is green, grown in the Caucasus. It is spooned generously, three pinches to a standard six-cup pot. And there is no question of leaving your table until you have drained the last of it.

Drinking, in such circumstances, becomes almost a form of meditation. The tea comes so scalding not even the thirstiest can gulp it down. You have to proceed as if it were a hot towel, rather than a cup, you are lifting to your face. With each sip you adjust a bit more to the glare, the searing heat, the turbans and caftans and vests surrounding you.

By now the tea may be drinking you more than you are drinking it. Water, always so precious—life itself, a neighbor maintains—is coursing through your body. You feel your body spreading to meet its flow, becoming one with your sleeves, with the life circulating around you. With the trees and the heat and the piercing music, conversation may be too difficult to attempt. But that doesn't keep you from admiring the yellow-and-white-striped shirt across from you. Not only are its stripes broader than anything on Bond Street, but it also has a diagonal band of yellow cut to emphasize that seat of male prosperity, the paunch.

The bed table you are dining on is a real bed, only bigger than most—for six. With carved metal designs on three sides, it resembles a campaign bed. The legs are high enough that dangling feet don't touch the ground. The diner does not squat so much as sprawl, Roman fashion, leaning back on a surveying elbow, letting a leg jut out.

When you are suspended on this flying carpet, exchanges happen differently than when seated face-to-face on chairs, legs solidly planted. Who you are is less important than the ongoing picture being created between you. I'm that odd bird, a private traveler. Most foreigners who descend on Bukhara are package tourists. No sooner has their bus delivered them than it is scooping them up. Even when the bus is parked, the motor is always running, as if at any moment the bus might take off. On their faces you see the panic it inspires: not so much the fear of being left—in the Soviet Union no one is ever left behind—but of holding up the others, upsetting finely tuned schedules. They are, they can only be, their cameras, and you see them, behind departing bus windows, feverishly clicking away.

A traveler with a pen and a packet of lined note cards is a different kettle of fish. Seizing the opportunity, I may even haul out these tools of my trade—the equivalent of their awl? their silversmith's pliers? In a moment, such is the mercantile spirit of the place, they weigh in with offers for my watch, my sneakers, my trousers. Surely in jest—they can't expect me to disrobe on the spot—but secretly I feel flattered. Were Bukhara my final port of call, I might well oblige them—anything to lighten a suitcase.

———

Once you have visited and revisited the great monuments, what do you do with the rest of your time? Visit the Desert National Park, advertised by a camel poster in the hotel lobby? Well, you are told, the desert park is no longer in operation. "What does that mean?" a friend asks, outraged. "Have they trucked it off to Siberia?" A desert that won't someday bloom, even one of the scope of the Kyzyl Kum, must be intolerable to the Soviet imagination.

When all else fails there is the bazaar. On a Sunday, with a quarter of a million bargainers flooding in from all over, there is nothing quite like it. Spread out on cloths, on fold-up aluminum cots, on fenders of carpet-draped trucks, for much of a square mile a commercial labyrinth sells everything from food and clothing to household appliances. In the noon glare and in the absence of even an awning, it's pretty impressive.

The pressure of milling crowds, of vendors squatting at your feet, goods pegged at every conceivable eye level, turns you into a cog being shunted along, up one barely bodywide aisle and down the next. The proximity offers an opportunity to gawk: at the fronts and backs, beards, wispy Mongolian moustaches, caps, and shawls of your fellow shoppers; and best of all, at the vendors, who, here at least, are spared Soviet canons of dress. The women are in their most outrageous five-piece outfits, pattern clashing against pattern—why match when, with a little courage, you can elate?

Pulled by a gingerly shuffling current, I have time enough to grasp the different pieces that make up an outfit. The old, beautiful-eyed women vendors patiently seated on the ground are the usual paisley-shawled flowers. Younger ones favor a costume more strikingly dissonant. This national sunburst, as I think of it, may come in any one of a number of background colors—black, green, whatever. Soon I see that what appear to be bands of printed vertical stripes are actually patterns of flowing pendants in which a zebralike band of black and yellow drops onto a band of red only to revert to black and yellow and then white—lightning flashes zigzagging down to the knees.

Even this vibrant clash of stripes and color pales before the sheer resonance of the women's bloomers. Visible only from the knee down, these bloomers form the centerpiece of a lady's costume, her fashion statement at its most chic. Add a vest, or a long coat with silver-filigreed sleeves, and set it off with a strand or two of jingling, dangling breast ornaments, and she is what one might call dressed.

For men, especially those sporting the traditional shaved skull, fashion turns on the quest for the ultimate box cap. Compared to the magnificence of a turban, a cap may seem pedestrian. But one is not shelling out for eighteen meters of silk. And a cap in summer must be a sight cooler than the fur towers the Turkomans parade about in. But caps seem to get worn out awfully fast. Wherever I turn, there are groups of men, or a man and his wife, looking them over, turning them inside out to examine the stitching. Clearly, nothing less than a man's dignity is at stake.

Over kohl-rimmed eyes and long braids, women often wear similar caps. Theirs come in a wider color range than the men's black and white. Covered with shawls, they make their heads into little mountains.

To the extent your feet are free, you may move forward, drawn wherever there is a crowd. What new has fallen off the back of a truck? Why of course, children's plastic shoes! To a roll of drums, in the middle of a ring of spectators, a strongman is lying on his back—don't I want to add my bulk to that of those trying to crush him? A dozen or more of us take up positions on a board straddling his chest until the drum rolls again and we hop down to go our separate ways.

In an earlier life, the parchment paper, made out of rags, might have tempted me. Or the silver decorated with glass mounted on colored paper that makes it all sparkle. Or, the height of feminine elegance, the gold-embroidered dresses still encountered of an evening by the Liabi Hauz pool. Every now and then from a booth a song wafts irresistibly, and the disk must be bought. Here is an old silver knife, at thirty dollars hardly a bargain. But with my pockets stuffed with unnegotiable rubles it's worth a hesitant gulp. Aside from old, luxuriously fringed silk shawls, what attracts me are neckties. They come already knotted, with an elastic band to go under the collar. I buy one of a rich peacock blue splashed with sequins. If this is the one bit of fantasy men are permitted, what says it more persuasively?

In shopping, I am not just buying *things,* I am buying something that has been part of a vendor's life. As I pass one nonagenarian, she thrusts up a little boy's embroidered blue-and-gold jacket with a gesture that could not be clearer: "Isn't this exactly what you have your heart set on?" I couldn't agree more and, squatting beside her, extend my pad so there's no misunderstanding about the price. But the vendor hails from a time before they taught writing, so a girl from a neighboring stand comes to our rescue. Numbers are dutifully written down, hers, mine, ping-pong. I pay and the girl kindly makes change for us. By the time I have finished thanking her, the old lady has vanished, the notes tucked into her bodice. For how many Sundays I don't know, she has had her eye fixed on a purchase of her own, and now that she has the wherewithal, she has gone to claim it.

By now it's early afternoon and the heat has everyone packing up. For those loath to scramble for a taxi, there is the covered fruit-and-vegetable market. High in a tree over the main gateway invisible caged birds chirp away. Dried fruit—apricots of every shade of gold, raisins as tasty as any on earth—lies so copiously piled that, going from pile to pile, one can make a small lunch. Last year's pomegranates are still available, along with hut-high mounds of watermelons. There are even dried apricot pits and melon seeds that, ground into a paste, make a flat cake.

After the heat of the bazaar, a visit to the public baths seems in order. Armed with the word, *hammam,* and an illustrative towel, I set off through the labyrinth. Eventually I find it, a multidomed building, with separate entrances for males and females.

At this hour it is uncrowded; an attendant makes sure I don't enter the bath without a towel. I use it as I would a washcloth, lathering myself with soap from a portable basin. For water, there are two showers and various spigots that, properly tapped, sputter forth. All around steam is rising, so thick that the steps leading to a second sauna room are invisible. But I see a wraith descending them and up I go for considerably hotter steam. When I return, unaccustomed eyes blinking at the light, I notice a score of corpulent figures spread out on one or another tile bench. They are all waiting to be kneaded. Someone pummels away at back and shoulders and then the pummeled one returns the favor. The rest of us sit, so many large turtles, heaving, dripping, until dry enough to venture into the now welcome air.

———————

On my last afternoon a Soviet journalist from Tass does me the honor of an interview for the local paper. Lenin's birthday is two days away, so I'm asked about him and the approaching Reagan-Gorbachev summit. By way of news, he tells me that the Afghan question has been solved in Geneva.

"Solved," I remark, "only as far as America and the Soviet Union are concerned—what about the Afghans?"

Finally comes the summarizing question, "What, by way of friendship, do you wish for the people of Central Asia?"

By this time I seem to have lost any volubility I may have once possessed. A single word stands out for me and, unable to help myself, I let it fly: "Autonomy."

There is a pronounced silence. Perhaps *autonomy* is not a word in the Soviet lexicon? But the word, as it turns out, does translate. What bothers him, as a fellow writer, is the lack of a mediating adjective. "What sort of autonomy?" he asks.

For the life of me, I can't wish for this conquered people anything but a complete restoration of their religion, their culture, their whole historic identity—and on this inarticulate note my stay in Bukhara ends.

KHIVA

The way to arrive in Khiva is, of course, by caravan. After twenty days spent crossing the infamous Kara Kum Desert, the City of Nightingales must have looked the very image of paradise. Not even in Germany, the early-nineteenth-century traveler Muraviev remarked, had he seen countryside so intensively cultivated. Yet even its "numberless" gardens were quickly eclipsed by the towering monuments of the walled inner city. In the twenty-two-hectare enclosure of the Ichan Qala—nearly all of one period (1780 to 1850)—the theatricality that every Central Asian city aimed at is realized to an unprecedented degree.

If you can't arrive by caravan, next best might be by train from Bukhara. The Kyzyl Kum Desert may not quite rank with the Kara Kum, but two days and a night might acquaint one with a variety of Turkmenian presences. And the great vacancies with their sensuous dunes and gaunt *saksaul* elms might remind one of how close the Russian conquerors of Khiva in 1874, General Kaufmann and his army, came to perishing, to be saved by a scout's chance discovery of a well fifty miles away. So, when Intourist told me in Moscow I'd be arriving by train, I was elated. In most countries, trains have a limited curiosity value. In the Soviet Union, they offer a celebration of life akin to what I had known following the twenty-two-day Tour de France bicycle race.

Alas, when my schedule came through, I learned I was arriving by air. The train, I was told, was not a good one, with only four sleeping compartments. And the heat, even in April, was stifling. Mother Intourist may have been right in sparing me discomfort. But her real motive, I suspect, was financial. The agency would not be earning hard currency while I was touring the Kyzyl Kum courtesy of USSR Railways.

So there I was, plopping down on modern Urganch, where I was required to stay, a soulless city built on the Stalinist monster block model, some forty minutes by car from Khiva. (There was a hotel in Khiva converted from a religious academy, but it was for Russians only.) "What! No group?" the airport taxi driver asked, fixing on the pariah a look of the most withering scorn, a look that left me wondering how, by myself, I was to arrange the daily commute to Khiva.

There were, I found, public conveyances I could take. Seventy-five passengers crammed with all their effects onto a forty-five-seat bus was a bit cozy. But it was instructive to see, as we passed a cemetery, every one of them dropping their bundles to run both hands over their faces in a traditional Muslim gesture. Obviously, Big Brother wasn't watching.

The gardens and orchards with their nightingales may have vanished for the nonce—cotton is even more prevalent than in Bukhara—but the three-mile walk from the bus terminal by the old city gate to the Ichan Qala revealed tree-lined streets and canals such as I had never encountered in a Central Asian town. But the houses' north-facing courtyards, with their tall, slanted, three-quarter-covered roofs, foretold the summer heat I was being spared.

The scale and coherence of effect of the massively walled inner city impressed me: six great towers lined up on a single axis; vast entrance portals made even bigger by the raised platforms out of which their facades loomed, dropping abruptly onto a sunken alley, a street twisting every which way to catch every possible particle of wind and shadow. As I walked, every few steps threw out new perspectives, of great domes, tree-shaded squares, views plunging over the walls onto the belt of surrounding green. As Central Asian theater goes, this was it.

Yet the mood emanating from the buildings was a wary severity, a reminder of Khiva's garrison origins and, more chillingly, of the violence of the slave trade on which its prosperity was based.

Khiva came into being in the tenth century as a desert fortress protecting the caravan trail that linked the huge city of Merv and its million and a half population with the Aral Sea. The Ichan Qala first developed as the inner fortress. For oasis dwellers, it afforded refuge during periods of internecine warfare. For rulers, it served as a stronghold against any popular insurrection.

At the time the capital of the Khwārizm region was Urganch, an earlier Urganch that was situated two hundred kilometers from the present-day Urganch where I was staying. The Moroccan traveler Ibn Battūtah called it the "greatest, most beautiful and most important city of the Turks." What awed him when he visited it in 1331 was the seething mass of pedestrian throngs, "whose swaying movements lent it the semblance of a billowy sea." As a center of religious studies, Urganch was surpassed only by Bukhara. (Among its luminaries was the mathematician al-Khwārizmī, to whom we owe square roots and quadratic equations.) The oasis was long famed for the quality of its melons. Even in this century they were still being wrapped in individual leather cases and sent out on camels to adorn the tables of princes.

Such prosperity attracted looters. Genghis Khan razed Urganch in 1221, despite a heroic twelve-day resistance by twelve thousand men against a horde of six hundred thousand. Timur razed it no less than five times, surely a world record. By then he was so exasperated that he had the remaining inhabitants carted away as slaves and ordered barley to be sown over the city streets.

It was Urganch's vulnerability to the Amu Darya River that eventually spelled its doom. Endless travelers have attested to the filth and stench brought by the river's flooding. More devastating was the river's tendency to shift its banks—as much as sixty kilometers—leaving the inhabitants no recourse but to follow. The capital was finally abandoned in the seventeenth century.

By then Khiva was developing what would eventually become the largest slave market in Central Asia—the outgrowth of a symbiotic relationship between oasis inhabitants and surrounding nomads. Khwārizm's nomads were Turkomans who had migrated east out of Anatolia at the end of the ninth century. It was perhaps only natural that a people famous to this day for their falcons, furs, swift horses, and beautiful carpets should develop a trade in human bodies. A household's slave business lay in extracting a variety of whimpers and groans: an ear or finger stub that, when put into an envelope and entrusted to a caravan, might secure a quick ransom. While traveling, Vambéry lived in constant fear of having his disguise penetrated and sharing their fate. His harrowing account relates the considerable variety of tortures visited on captives as a matter of business. But families are not all equally solicitous about their kidnapped members, so the slave market developed as a way of disposing of the unransomable.

Every now and then, slaves succeeded in revenging themselves. A famous instance occurred in 1715, when the khan, after a battle against a Persian force, found himself with a surfeit of prisoners. Since Persians were the acknowledged master craftsmen of Central Asia, the khan decided to have all this talent build him a boarding school where he could house the Russian mission being sent by Peter the Great. The Persians agreed, on the condition they be allowed to return to their homes once the school was finished. But the khan was so taken by the elegance of their craftsmanship that he began to have second thoughts about repatriating such a valuable work force. Perhaps, before departing, they could build him a summer palace? The khan's reneging, as can be imagined, did not go over very well. One day, as he was hemming and hawing, one of the Persians picked up a brick, the others followed, and before anyone could intervene, the khan had been stoned to death.

The Russian emissaries, meanwhile, had been making their way across the saltscapes. They arrived to find a new khan installed. For the life of him he could not make head or tail of the secret negotiations Peter the Great's envoys kept referring to. In a fit of exasperation, he decapitated them all and sent their heads back on an enormous silver platter to the czar.

Here matters rested until 1740, when the last great Persian conqueror, Nāder Shāh, arrived at the head of a considerable army. A Turkoman himself who had murdered five brothers on the way to the Peacock Throne, Nāder Shāh was determined to abort a slave trade that flourished mainly at his subjects' expense. The razing he inflicted was such that, even twenty years later, there were a scant forty families living in Khiva and wild animals prowled the ruins.

In Central Asia, cities rise from their ashes remarkably fast. By the end of the century Khiva's irrigation system had been restored, bazaars built, and trade opened with Bukhara, Persia, and Russia. The new prosperity was again based on the slave trade, busier now than ever. From Persia alone, in the first half of the nineteenth century, a million people were snatched. Khiva itself had fifty to sixty thousand slaves. Fueled by this labor pool, the modern Ichan Qala came into being. Just as a J. P. Morgan or a Rockefeller might salve his conscience by endowing a university or a civic auditorium, so did the khan's merchants and generals vie in erecting religious academies. In the Ichan Qala there are twenty-two such academies, roughly one per hectare. That's a lot of physical plant.

In Samarkand and Bukhara there are distinctive Central Asian decorative techniques, but the finished product is by and large Persian inspired. In Khiva, what strikes me are the changes in the basic vocabulary and the signal confidence the buildings generate. Something new is at work.

Take the tile paneling. Compared to Bukhara and Samarkand, colors are quite restricted. There are no reds, oranges, greens, yellows, blacks. Even turquoise intrudes only as a highlight, an odd teardrop on the ribbing of an arch. Khiva, in effect, is not thinking color so much as design where medallion tile panels play off against their borders. The panels are remarkably varied. In the whole of the Royal Court one rarely finds two alike.

The medallion design may have sprung from any number of sources, even a manual brought back from a pilgrimage. There may well be some crossover from the allied art of wood carving, which reaches a subtlety in Khiva unsurpassed in Central Asia. The Winter Mosque's great forest of columns, many of them saved from the ruins of Urganch, may have given tile craftsmen a repertoire of forms on which to draw.

If sources resist being pinned down, much of the credit rests with one man, Abdallah Djinn. (*Djinn* suggests that his designs had a bit of the devil in them.) Whenever a tile panel is particularly striking you can be sure that he, or his brother, was the designer.

Abdallah's masterpiece was the Pahlavan Makhmoud Mausoleum (1810 to 1825), built to commemorate a twelfth-century poet and undefeated wrestler who hailed from the same Koungrat family as the ruling khan. Makhmoud was a writer of rubaiyat deeply influenced by Omar Khayyām. The verse inscribed on his tomb testifies to a life of a certain frustration:

It is far easier to spend a hundred years in jail,
to climb a hundred mountains,
than to persuade a stupid man of the truth.

Not very democratic, perhaps. But anyone who has put in time teaching may recognize the sentiment.

In the earlier tile work of Samarkand and Bukhara, designs conjure an image of the afterlife seen as a spring meadow. Faith insists that it go on and on, across one wall or arch to the next. It is not individual flowers, but the play of color we see, an ever changing kaleidoscope of blue, green, orange, red. Behind this outburst of color, of dawn, of floral waves lit and dancing, we can't help but be aware of the single held breath which miraculously contains it and places it within a greater rhythm. The tiles depict, in other words, the garden of faith, the paradise awaiting the illuminated believer.

The same belief system extends to the gardens and night skies Abdallah conjures up, where the design is no longer a static one, but a restless swirl pulling me every which way at once. The effect of these starflowers is less of inescapable profusion than of almost musical speed. And nothing in the framing architecture is allowed to get in the way of dizzying, vertiginous movement. Indented archways, we feel, exist for form's sake only. They are tiny by comparison with what we have seen elsewhere, and the corners where they are placed are so low the eye is encouraged to vault over them to the great gonglike medallions of the six-triangled dome. It's less a hypnotic effect Abdallah is conjuring up than one of amazement, to which has been added a hint of darkness, of the mystical awe a star-studded canopy can induce.

Abdallah Djinn also had a hand in the Ichan Qala's Tash Hauli. A fort within the fort of the Royal Court, the 163-room stone palace features a series of strongholds, complete with turrets and crenellated walls, within a series of separately enclosed compounds.

The fate of the khan's primary architect, Nour, is another story. All the khan wanted from Nour was a palace larger and more sumptuous than anything extant in Central Asia. With so many slaves about, he must have thought that all Nour had to do was crack a whip to have it finished in two years at most. As months dragged on with no prospect of his being able to move in, the khan became impatient. A contract is a contract! He insisted that the architect pay with his head if the palace were not finished on time. When Nour bravely protested it wasn't feasible, not even with the whole city working day and night, the khan, a ruler of his word, had him executed. Even so, it was another ten years before the palace was finished in 1840.

Most of the Tash Hauli was still being restored, work that was expected to continue for several more years, and it was possible to view only the harem. You enter by way of a courtyard the size of a small soccer field designed to accommodate the round felt tents in which the inhabitants passed the winter. Off it are five open-fronted blue-tiled receiving rooms, their painted ceilings supported by marble-based carved wooden columns. Each room leads off into a private boudoir. Lining the courtyards are horizontal panels of blue-and-white tile strewn like carpets, a calm background for the colors of silken costumes, the sounds of plucked instruments, and the inevitable dancing.

Immediately after the Tash Hauli was completed, the khan decided to erect nearby a skyscraperlike tower. This was the Kalta Minar, variously known as the Short or Green Tower. Judging by the 1908 Islam-Khoja Watchtower that replaced it, the Kalta Minar probably served a sentinel function. One can imagine how useful a tower of its eclipsing size might be in receiving messages from garrison outposts, in spotting caravans and raiding parties, and, not least, in keeping tabs on the comings and goings of the local citizenry.

No sooner was the word out than the khan's rival, the emir of Bukhara, was heard wanting a spy-in-the-sky of just those heaven-kissing dimensions, those radiantly changing greens and blues. As legend has it, he invited the tower's master builder to come to Bukhara for discussions. Unfortunately, news of the offer leaked out, and the khan was understandably peeved. You don't go to the trouble and expense of erecting the world's mightiest tower to see it pirated by your hated rival. The only fit response was to have his betrayer thrown from the tower's unfinished top.

The master builder somehow survived the fall, in what condition we are not told. Ordinarily, such a survival would be interpreted as an act of God. But the khan was not about to let the miscreant limp off to Bukhara. Instead he had him hauled once again to the top of the tower and thrown off. This was too much for the Kalta Minar's workmen. They walked out, and nobody of sufficient talent was ever found to replace them. The glory the completed tower might have reached—the blues and greens are just starting to come into their own—is tantalizing to imagine. Yet even in its drumlike state it remains the most arresting structure on the Khiva skyline.

———————————

Samarkand had capitulated in the 1850s; Bukhara, in 1868. Finally, in 1873, it was Khiva's turn. Sensing the end of an era, correspondents from all over Christendom descended on the city to cover the event. Some, like the Englishman David Ker, never made it, thanks to the terrain. But that did not keep Ker from publishing *On the Road to Khiva,* complete with photographs and a military map. The *New York Herald*'s John MacGahan did make it, and the sprightly account of his solo ride, *Campaigning on the Oxus and the Fall of Khiva,* went into three editions and to this day remains a travel classic.

Thus fell the last bastion of Central Asia; or rather, the next-to-last, as it was only in 1881, after a hard-fought siege, that the Turkmenian fortress of Geok Tepe was finally taken.

Once a theater's lights have dimmed it may be a while before they can be turned on again. But, within their limited mandate, the Soviets have certainly tried. While one may not much care for their way of creating a *cordon sanitaire* sealing off the great sets from any vestige of their century-rich life, one can't help being impressed by the scale of public resources and the thoroughness of the work committed to restoration. Samarkand, Bukhara, and Khiva are not yet the garden cities our imaginations require. But a number of historically important sites have been saved from oblivion. It even seems possible that, when the curtain lifts again, autonomy may return without recourse to the violence that originally brought these great cities into being.

AFTERWORD

Much of the text of "Samarkand, Bukhara, Khiva" came into being as a direct response to the liberalization Gorbachev introduced in the name of glasnost. In the same spirit, Abbeville Press felt they should attempt to promote a better understanding of what the new Soviet Union was about. To that end, they signed up the Ansel Adams of the Soviet Union, Vadim Gippenreiter, to do (among other volumes) a book on Central Asia. Looking at my "Persian Mirages," they thought that, with Gippenreiter's photographs in mind, I could travel there and capture the spirit of the newly open cities.

Gippenreiter had survived the Moscow purges of 1938, probably because he was an athlete. Indeed, he became the 1940 Soviet downhill ski champion. He wanted to be a sculptor and was enrolled in the Moscow Art Institute when, as a result of the Nazi advance, the institute was closed down and everyone evacuated to Samarkand, two time zones away in Central Asia. During his enforced stay in Samarkand, Gippenreiter discovered photography. He had already begun to see what being a Soviet sculptor meant: doing monumental busts of holy figures, as he called them—Lenin, Stalin, and their ilk—was not the career he saw for himself. Thus he became the Soviet Union's premier architectural photographer, an art form not all that far from sculpture.

Gippenreiter fell in love with Samarkand. He returned to photograph nearly every year and almost married a Tajik woman. "University background and very well connected," Vadim told me when we met in the Moscow apartment he shared with his painter son. "Had we married, I'd be a rich man today. But she didn't want to move to Moscow and I didn't want to spend the rest of my working life in Central Asia."

I tried to persuade Gippenreiter to accompany me to the three great cities; after all, the book needed his reflections on what he had shot. But he had a project on the churches of Little Russia to complete before a deadline. As he remarked, the light in spring was too murky when compared to the 120-degree glories of late summer, the almost daily weddings, and the mountains of produce in the bazaars.

That left me no alternative but to be my own eyes. Three weeks is not very much time, and much eluded me. I never, for instance, set foot inside anyone's house. But I did, I think, catch a moment, and I hope that my text, for all the political changes that subsequently occurred, still stands up.

Trinidad: Rain Forest Birding
1989

For encapsulating the memory of a day, a place, a streak of light, there is nothing like bird-watching. First, a taut readiness, glasses primed, as you stand waiting for a sound, a rustle, the least motion. Then the bird alights, in light, and, shocked, you will remember it all: the angle of the sun, the branch, the sky, the shape of the tree. A whole complex is forever part of you.

Bird-watchers who get spoiled don't want one bird, but lots of them, migrating flocks that blow in overnight and settle in the lot next door. But such storm-blown moments of utter plenitude, such miracles of number, of color washing in and out of the most unlikely branches, don't occur often, and it may be necessary to pursue migrations farther and farther afield. To the northeast tip of Mallorca in the first week of May, or Iceland in late June. For the truly obsessed, the ultimate fix must be South America, a continent that is to birds what East Africa is to animals. Colombia alone holds ten times as many species as all of Europe.

Traveling to Colombia and plunging cold into a large country's bewildering tropical variety seemed all too daunting. Better an island like Trinidad, where I could familiarize myself with a new vocabulary of antbirds, woodcreepers, motmots, manakins, and other families. By Venezuelan standards, the four hundred or so species recorded in Trinidad may not seem all that many, but that's one species for each five square miles. And the island boasts a number of oddities, such as oilbirds, bellbirds, and manakins, that are not easily come by on the continent.

To identify it all, I carried Richard French's copious guide, *The Birds of Trinidad and Tobago,* and D. W. Snow's beautifully written study of manakins, oilbirds, and cotingas, *A Web of Adaptation.* And I had cabled in advance to a small birders' hotel in Saint Benedict Parish requesting a room.

Such green settlements! I remember thinking as I peered out of the descending airplane window. A rugged bump later and there I was, let out into a confusion of taxi drivers. What had kept the island's multiracial powder keg from exploding now that oil prices had dropped was hard to say, but signs of the new snatch-and-grab economy could not have been more evident: pacing Dobermans and tiers of receding locks and grilles, behind which everyone was obliged to sleep.

The cab driver, after asking what had drawn me—I did not feel I could say an adolescent addiction to off-color calypso—refused to take me to Saint Benedict.

"There are no birds there. All they've got is fires, from the squatters burning up the trees." He persuaded me I'd do better to stay at the Asa Wright Nature Center in the still-forested northern part of the island. A former plantation (coffee, cocoa, citrus fruit), it had been left to return to rain forest.

Once at the nature center, it took a while before any rain forest bird let me view it. In the forest stillness, a new footstep, the mere crackling of a branch, ripples out over a radius of hundreds of yards, and any bird hearing it takes appropriate evasive action. Songs, when they resume, rarely indicate anyone visible. With predators about, birds will sing only from a point of concealment, and the more operatic the call, the deeper the concealment.

Oh, there were oropendolas—huge black birds with yellow tails and beaks—crashing their thunderous wings and emitting surprising Japanese water-gardenlike *tocks* as they flew from one pendulous woven nest to the next. But in the forest the rule was stillness, punctured every now and then by the apparition of a mixed flock of ten or even twenty different species, each from a different plate in the bird guide, who would vanish before I could focus enough to figure out who they were.

Nothing here like a goldfinch pumping across a meadow or a magpie rowing itself, gondolierlike, from one treetop to the next. The norm was the bananaquit, zipping about at nothing less than rocket speed. How I envied watchers more experienced, for whom a hanging shape, a silhouette in flight, were name enough. Or those with ears good enough to resolve the understory's twitterings and calls into the distinct instruments of a forest orchestra. Instead, I found myself taken in by the fluttery acrobatics of a falling leaf or by a coppery remnant on a high bough that resembled a perched hummingbird.

In the rain forest, food is so abundant that a male can take care of his minimum daily requirements in less than an hour. What does he do with the rest of the day? Some, like the bellbird, head off to a favorite singing perch high in the forest leafage, flexing their facial wattles for as much as eight hours at a stretch. Others, like the white-bearded manakin, prefer a communal sports field, or *lech,* as it's known, doing something akin to what we kids used to do running bases in the sand—an image that hardly does justice to the dexterity with which the manakins go into action upon the arrival of a female spectator, puffing out their pillow-white throats and clicking their wings as they speed around a set of stumps, emitting a noise like the cracking of nuts.

Antbird convocations are even more noisy. If in the middle of an otherwise silent forest you become aware of a small racket— not unlike the clatter of knives and forks and the popping of champagne corks at a banquet—it's more than probable that army ants are out marching. The noise comes from antbirds' excitement at the delicious variety of insect life tossed in all directions by a single-minded ant colonnade.

"Hey, see what I've got! Come over here!" Antwrens, ant-vireos, spinetails, streaked xenops, a whole family the likes of which you have never seen before, all trying to make their particular excitement heard above the din. Watching them judiciously hopping about, just out of range of the ants, I sense their pride in the army that vacuums their forest floor.

After a few days in the forest, my ear progressed to where I could break down woodpecker morse into specific resonances; separate, say, the clear major of a cocoa thrush's whistle from the Haydnesque minor of the white-necked thrush. Rather than strain my eyes, I would wait for a swift to bank before declaring it gray rumped or band tailed. A turning, a twisting in air, willing the wind to itself, yes, that must be a sand martin. Then there were parrots, always in pairs, round winged and making such hard work of it; not so much flying, from what I could tell, as doing laps, side by side, up and down the great green pool of a valley.

Always before, I told birds using binoculars, skimming hither and thither on the water of the light, while picking up telltale markings of cap, eyebrow, lores, or rump. In the forest once, randomly scanning, I managed to land on a rare spadebill, riding out noon in a cleft between two trunks. Easier is the jacamar, a pink-throated kingbird-size hummingbird look-alike in a heavily sequined, tightly clinging copper-green gown, always hanging out where I don't expect it, in the shade a couple of feet off the ground, where sequins are less apt to alarm a passing dragonfly. Even more rewarding are the trogons of the midstory, birds that never appear without an oval portrait frame. For whole minutes they will sit, so still I can find bristles surrounding the beak, the pale blue eye-ring within the dark blue head. But most of the time it is the volume of sound, and to a sharper degree its placement, the height and distance it is being poured out from, that tells who the bird is and where to begin looking.

Because of the high caloric intake singing requires, much territorial assertion takes place in the cool of early morning and immediately before or after sudden downpours. This also explains why many of the more intelligent birds—parrots, oropendolas, ravens—chatter away with hundreds of calls, without attempting the sustained output of song.

In the darkness of first light, the forest can seem a tide of accumulating song. As one dies out, another takes its place—like a game of tag, played at every pitch conceivable, each acting as if his voice alone stimulated the dawn to ever redder efforts. In the density all around, I could hear them noisily flapping, but the only visible silhouettes belong to the sky's parrots and herons, who are heading toward their own invisibilities.

In lowland heat, such intensity does not last long; it's best to have a good viewing spot staked out when the first blaze of light gets kicked downfield. When I got there in time, I could watch the big-eyed, slow-moving night shift of owls, nightjars, toads, and snakes, all scurrying to get back to their roosts before the day team thunders in. At dawn quickness is everything, the quickness to seize what light reveals, before the defenses, the camouflage, are finally adjusted.

Once the day gets hot, all a bird can do is ride it out hidden under a leaf, willing its heartbeat to a *slow* dissolve. There is occasional mournful cooing, but I wonder, all teasing aside, what it represents. Is it a ground dweller's way of ventilating itself in the heat, a kind of repeated *om* to propel itself from one dappled bit of leaf litter to the next?

To this, the bellbird is an exception. Even at noon I hear him, a young male, practicing that penetrating hammer-hitting-metal bonk he is bent on mastering. But where? I wonder, as the trail moves up, then down over a tiny bridge and around an abandoned manakin *lech*. With each step I become that much more open to brook sounds, fluttering leaves, wind, and the tiniest vocal disturbance. Arrows of light strike into the density where the young male is singing, where one or another leaf, briefly illuminated, quivers. Then someone who has better aural placement spots him.

"See where that shaft of light is catching the palm frond? There, just four feet above and slightly to the left, is the bellbird we've been hearing."

I understand the spotter's excitement. This sight, of a bird so uncompromisingly vocal, with his three indescribable black facial wattles, begs to be shared; one can't go so deep into the forest and return without it. Meanwhile there I am, down in the dimness, with not a clue to where that shaft of light over the palm frond they are talking about might possibly be until, by sheer happenstance, I light on the apprentice, high in the leafage, bonking himself forth into the midstory's gloom. Such energy! Such persistence! And I wonder what it would be like to sit there and watch him with his black wattles, hour after hour, day after day, coming closer to getting right the extraordinary song that will be his male advertisement.

The higher I climb in the forest, the more visually spectacular the bird life. There was one fig tree near the crest of a mountain that must have been the avian equivalent of a three-star restaurant. There alone, I spotted a toucan, several species of thrush, all three trogons, a female bellbird, and all the tanagers that had eluded me so far. The female bellbird, a streaked grouse-size creature, was so weighed down by all she had eaten as to be virtually immobilized, unable for all our racket to fly away. She became a point of reference: "at two o'clock, above the bellbird." Of the tanagers, the last to come into view, the so-called speckled, summed up in its extravagant plumage the whole mountain scene: wings of an ethereal pale blue contrasted with a pale green body subtly tinged with yellow; the whole of it, in a kind of frantic afterthought, "Aren't I somewhat too vulnerable?" repainted in a confusion of black dots and wing dashes. Paradise, but staccato, in the leaf shadows, feeding.

Many tropical forests are dense enough that you can easily get lost if you step off the trail. But in Trinidad, you can wander about from one copse to the next. The rain forest's real enemy is not fire, but wind. For all the buttressing of projecting roots, the trees, piled one on top of the other and reaching to the top of the mountain, are little more than a house of cards. Since leaf litter either washes away or is instantly consumed, there isn't much in the way of soil to grip. That may be why many trees tolerate parasite vines that will outstrip and eventually choke them. Whatever else, parasites offer protection from wind. With enough insulation, trees can concentrate on the business of creating moisture, the constant splash of notes that is the mark of a true forest.

Thirty miles out to sea from Trinidad is the island of Tobago. As a newcomer, I wanted to contrast the bird life of the two islands. But I should have known better than to come in April, when squatter farmers are busy setting the fields ablaze. The winter had been one of the driest on record and the burners were making the most of it. They needed, they claimed, combustion to destroy insects and vermin and get decent yields. But on newly bare hillsides, nothing prevents humus from being washed away, and the absence of brush only adds to aridity.

The burning is illegal, and every day there were admonishments on television, pointing out ecological hazards and the virtues of terracing. But, like many governments in the Third World, Tobago's is better at writing laws than enforcing them. I met one warden who, in eighteen years on the job, had not made a single arrest. As a bureaucrat, he found it demeaning to be asked to behave like a police officer.

As for the squatters, they have little interest in preserving the value of land not theirs, or in investing precious time to make terraces. Of course, the government could recognize a fait accompli and turn the squatters into owners; but expropriation is a slippery nut to grasp, especially for a government utterly dependent on foreign investment. Perhaps the burgeoning interest in ecotourism will lead to agricultural practices more friendly to wildlife, not to mention future generations. But walking about the hillsides of Tobago, in a stench of blackened earth, could hardly compare with the forest bird-watching I had enjoyed on Trinidad.

Indelible Gestures: New Guinea's Birds and Men

1993

To find the essence of Papua New Guinea, one should journey directly to the Central Highlands, where a third of the people and the most interesting birds dwell. But most visitors land in the sprawling modern capital, Port Moresby. At night the town resembles a minor war zone, full of the sounds of edgy tribesmen popping away at one another. There's no store of any size that does not feature a cudgel-wielding security guard (with a backup holding a German shepherd on a fist-thick rope). At night, with old tribal hatreds jostling one another, it's not where you want to be. There's no way to stamp out anarchy when each youth knows his clan people will kill any judge so rash as to sentence him.

Yet somehow or other the townspeople cope. Cities the world over make a point of preserving personal anonymity, but never before have I run into an entire population decked out in sunglasses. Where we hide inside pale cottons to try to protect ourselves from the worst equatorial rays, they embrace light, turning the streets into a fire-speak of skirt, beads, sneakers, hat. From my hotel window a beach seems a battlefield of red and blue, the odd pink as shocking as a flamingo. Out of nowhere each person appears as his own brilliant strike, such are the splashes of color, of shadow, he brings. A moment later, he has somehow vanished, leaving you with your hands raised in wonder.

Bird plumages were displayed well enough in the breathtakingly sharp light of Variata National Park's coastal highway overlooking Port Moresby, provided one had a telescope to reel them in. Without straying more than fifty yards, we must have noted seventy species. A single gigantic fig seemed less a tree than a continually changing kaleidoscope containing some forty of them, everything from three-inch parrots to gorgeously mottled imperial pigeons. Its fruit is a kind of Jacob's coat that provides the pectin birds need to take on color.

By no means were they all beautiful. There was a tribe of meliphaga honeyeaters distinguished from one another by nothing more salient than a paler, perhaps smaller ear spot, a thinner bill, the color of an iris or a rictal streak. But on first exposure to an utterly distinct Australasian bird life, I am struck by all the red plumages. An American cardinal or tanager would be lost in the crowd.

The deep trench that separates New Guinea from Southeast Asia has made for a unique evolutionary track. As Darwin's great contemporary Alfred Russel Wallace observed, New Guinea's wildlife differs more from that of nearby Malaysia than Malaysia's does from that of Africa and the neotropics. The birds' selections of plumage, voice, sexual and nesting strategies turn on an axis all their own. And it's an evolution that, with humans' help, is still progressing.

Of all the major islands, New Guinea is alone in not having suffered a twentieth-century avian extinction. From its forests, a number of the world's most beautiful and complex bird families have radiated out. Among them are kingfishers, parrots, bowerbirds, birds of paradise, and an array of subtly colored fruit doves and pigeons. The absence of primate and squirrel competition—bats and marsupials feed at night—has brought forth a plethora of fruit eaters. There's a different parrot for every size of branch, from the thinnest twig to the stoutest bough. Meanwhile human migration into towns has worked in the birds' favor. There is less pressure on them now than in at least a millennium—except along roads. Unlike Java, New Guinea has never had a trade in caged birds. The human population, under control everywhere but in the Central Highlands, numbers no more than four million. With the world's largest gold mine, vast reserves of oil, and most property still privately held, the nation may even have a viable future.

The extensive forests and folded landscape that make for a diversity of birds have also created a remarkable diversity of people and languages. In New Guinea there are 1,230 languages (720 in Papua New Guinea), representing 28 of the world's 55 language families. The people are Negroid in feature, but skin colors range from blond-haired Melanesians through hues of bronze, blue, or purple, all the way to a color-defying black that is like anthracite.

From studies in nearby New Britain, an island rich in obsidian, we have a fair idea how human settlement occurred. It is generally reckoned as dating from fifty thousand years ago— about the same time as the fig trees. Hunters from Southeast Asia drifted in, looking for wallabies and pigeons, and after wiping them out, moved on. Besides destroying the local wildlife, there are indications they may have contributed to it as well by releasing parrots and lorikeets. To this day, the relationship between people and birds remains very close. Yet, while every tribe possesses a full classification system, not everyone in a community has fallen under the birds' spell.

"There are so many," I remember a man telling me, "we've run out of words with which to tell them apart." But those who know birds are more than likely to know their vocalizations. In the case of the birds of paradise, New Guinea exhibits a unique instance of a parallel evolution between birds and people.

THE BENSBACH

Before savoring the distinctiveness of the Central Highlands, it makes sense to sample the ecosystems that lead up to it.

Accordingly, we start from an isolated lodge on the Bensbach River in the trans–Fly River region, an hour's flight southwest of Port Moresby, not far from the Irian border.

This is young country, where rivers run straight with hardly a bend. But the fickleness with which they erode their banks is hard on trees. Survival depends on getting the distance right: near enough for the roots to drink; far enough not to be swept away.

The forest here, a hundred feet above sea level, is a seasonally flooded savannah. Blink your eyes and you might well imagine yourself in an Africa of traveler palms and squat baobab trees, except the fleeing herds are not wildebeest and zebras, but hopping bandicoots and wallabies along with recently introduced deer. The terrain is dominated by palms and tall white-trunked trees whose thin red leaves glow like coins against gray earth. Invisible brush turkeys call out, giant lizards moan, and all too quickly a mixed species flock passes before I can figure out which name is where in the swirling group.

In open country, birds spend much of their time flying about; you can't wait for them to alight to identify them. When they do alight, chances are they will become instantly invisible: parrots crawl around in the foliage like lice, then shock you as a whole tree bursts into raucous flight. To tell them, you have to recognize profiles, ups and downs of flight, and type of wing flap, adding what you can distinguish of cries—the speeding chatter of a flight of lorikeets, the whistle, so melodic and full of confidence, of the beautiful butcher bird.

With its variety of trees and overhanging vine-matted thickets, the Bensbach makes for difficult viewing. For birds, the task is to find a plumage at one with the scorching glass on which they hunt. That's what a variety of tiny kingfishers have turned themselves into—electric blue river crystals. You come upon them sitting low over the water in all their intensity, sapphire stillnesses transparent as a watch, eyes that pierce like a dentist's drill. On snags, a line of egrets stand like sheets of linen set out to dry, making a white foreground that contrasts with a hamlet's peaked thatch roofs and twelve-foot-high garden stockades. A flock of royal spoonbills banks and turns over the river, catching the sun's rays before dissolving like so many white-and-roseate sequins in the distance. Then, while your glasses are still trained on them, the entire sky above fills with an eerie shadow—the great wings of a cruising sea eagle.

In our river boat we have several times come upon isolated pairs of very large brolga cranes promenading alongside one another, as if held by invisible twine, grace on a riverbank united. We wake at the one time of the day they call, a back-and-forth *boom* that, even in the heavy air, carries a good half mile. Then, one afternoon, as we round a river bend, we spot what seems the whole nation gathered in a flooded meadow. Docking out of sight, we walk single file across a swale, then vanish within a stand of casuarina trees. Not many feet away, feeding peacefully, are some two hundred cranes, well over four feet tall, gray with rust crowns and red striping around their beaks. Suddenly one lifts its head and starts fanning its wings. Preparatory to flight? But instead of taking off, there she stays, as if on stilts, bouncing up and down barely off the ground, like linen blown along in a gale.

A second crane feeding nearby feels impelled to join her. Facing one another and spreading wingtips upward like petals, in unison the two lift into the air and touch down. Then, still facing each other, they take to the air once more, only this time it's a good twelve feet and has every look of flight. Yet they aren't flying; they are doing the dream of flight we humans call dancing: a lank, suspended wing work—momentarily afloat—as if the round air contained a music sustaining their bodies as they balance, teetering, before sideslipping down. Again and again, never more than a house high, the two leap, flapping, until paired now, they fly away to seal their pas de deux. As I watch a succession of pairings off and indelible gestures, I feel I have experienced something of the envy, the need to emulate, that gave birth to our communal dances. Does ballet get any better?

KIUNGA

Kiunga, an hour's flight north of the Bensbach, is a frontier town near the Irian border. The rivers' serpentine bands indicate that the system is much older than that of the savannah and the forest more fully established. It may not be as cathedrally impressive as the dipterocarp-dominated forest of Malaysia. And with a mere 80 to 160 species of trees per hectare, it falls far short of the 550 recorded in the upper Amazon. But what it lacks in sheer grandeur and diversity, it makes up for in the gardenlike understory. Every step draws its own exclamation: the banding of tree bark; the painterly textures of moss, lichen, fungi; the complexity of a spider web; a heart-stopping butterfly; exquisite tree ferns and a welter of plants, any one of which would grace a conservatory.

Before unstrapping a bush knife and hacking your way in, though, it is wise to find out exactly whose hunting ground you may be lousing up. That the world's second largest island contains an intact rain forest has much to do with the land being owned, by and large, by smallholders. The source of the world's habitat destruction is not peasants and the population pressure they exert, but the greed of large landowners to maximize yield per acre and their intolerance for anything resembling a buffer zone. What holds for landowners holds equally for governments, who need to sell forests to pay for bureaucracies, new glass buildings—the visible show on which central power insists. People's smallholdings are usually too scattered to permit the clear-cutting that forest industries depend on.

A man whose livelihood depends on hunting can get incensed at the incursions of ecotourists. But once you have gained his permission, more than likely he will escort you himself. For him, his forest is as much a garden as a place to hunt, and he is only too happy to show you its treasures: the tree with its nest of miniature hornets to which you must give a wide berth; the bark of another species that, when struck, produces instant fire. (No one would think of setting out on an overnight hike without his "fire," wrapped in a leaf and tied with a vine.)

With their slingshots and poisoned arrows, the hunters have created the sudden hush that greets a small party entering the forest. One can, of course, hunker down on a log and wait for ghostly names—cassowary, ground pigeons, brush turkey, scrub hens—to start ringing through intensely folded mountain mist. But we cope by putting our faces out there and edging forward in hesitating, one-step-at-a-time wariness. So long, we believe, as we don't unduly startle them, the birds will accept us.

For people the color of shadow there can be no such illusion. At the first bird-note of alarm, they drop into a squat and, moving rapidly, weave in and out of the light, eyes about level with the first tier of branches. Because hunting has so sharpened their perceptions, they are able to tell from the merest cooing exactly how far away a pigeon is, up to two miles. What to me are heat blurs they perceive as silhouettes, presences.

Birds exist only because they have managed to confound their pursuers and not be turned into clothing, or matter for the stew. Among them are canopy specks who have mastered the art of safety in numbers, careening in great squadrons like the gorgeous red-yellow-green dusky lories we found crowding onto a branch so thickly they actually broke it.

Close to the forest floor live the masters of invisibility, the pittas; beautiful glowing invisibility if one has the luck to catch, as I never could, the sapphire flash of a shoulder patch in flight. But for the hunter whose land we were on, seeing a pitta was hardly a problem. Commanding us to "Stay where you are!" he set off at a run to emerge, a few minutes later, with a never-before-seen pitta in each hand!

Against such skill, birds make their adjustments. In New Guinea, the mixed-species flocks associate by color. There are the All-Blacks, the All-Browns, and the Blacks-and-Browns. Because the forest is not tall and dense, as in Malaysia, and the landmarks more obvious, the flocks progress like an onward-spinning wheel. There is never an obvious leader like the black drongo you can cue your glasses on, knowing the rest won't be far behind. Instead, the hub of the wheel is apt to be something like the yellow-breasted gerygone, a plain little thing the size of a kinglet. Survival comes first and, because the gerygone cries out and warns—much as a willet does—the rest of the flock sticks close to him.

Such nervousness in constantly dripping, very difficult terrain does not make for easy viewing. Between you and your quarry there are tangles of thicket and vines and verticals of trunk, jammed pell-mell together. A hundred feet up, at a neck-splitting 180 degrees, you are aware of a passing flock's chirp-ings, riflelike reports, and shuddered warnings. You can try playing a tape recording, but generic calls work only on certain species. When the telephone rings, do you always pick it up? In New Guinea, a good number are inclined to let it ring. Looking around at the headdresses and simmering pots, you can hardly blame them.

Soaking wet and unable to see more than a couple of feet in front, you creep forward in boots ill adapted to the mud and slippery logs you must traverse, envying bare feet, which are so much easier to wipe off than shoes, and a lot more durable. And they adhere better, too. Over the centuries their feet have developed toes that grip like fingers, with a flattened sole to lend firmer support. And the mud can be like quicksand. Step off a path and in a few moments you may be sunk up to your waist, requiring a bridge of hands to pull you out.

The full effect of human presence became apparent to us when, in a heavy rain, we took an open boat along the un-peopled Elevara River. In the whole day, we did not see a boat and only a single encampment of people in traditional grass skirts. Big birds were consequently abundant: koels, imperial pigeons, flight after flight of Blyth's hornbill, a species we had heard frequently but never seen. The river was too low to see the fabled crowned pigeons sunning themselves low in the trees. But twice over the water we did see the orange, yellow, and red flying sunset of a flame bowerbird, known until recently only from a single specimen.

When we started, the river was so low there were logs forty feet up, caught in the branches. The height of the banks made clambering up a messy business. Still, there were some real rewards. Alerted by a descending, decelerating tremolo, very slow and deep and soft, I picked out, deep in the understory, what looked like a red flower. The "flower" turned out to be the red beak of a paradise kingfisher with a brown head and black wings that changed into iridescent blue as it flew, flashing a long blue pennant tail. On an island where many species wander over hundreds of miles, the paradise kingfisher possesses one of the most restricted territories, never being found more than four hundred feet from its nest.

As impressive as the bird life were the brooklets and little waterfalls unleashed by the downpour. We returned using a forest cut that had been dry when we set out. In twelve hours, the Elevara had risen three feet.

THE CENTRAL HIGHLANDS

From Kiunga we ascended to Tabubil in the foothills of the Star Mountains, one of the wettest places on earth. (It rains every day without fail, 180 inches in the course of a year.) From Tabubil, we then flew along the Hindenberg Wall to Tari in the Central

Highlands. This great wall, in places a sheer nine thousand feet high, is responsible for isolating the highland area from the rest of New Guinea; it was not until 1935 that the first airplane-borne white men arrived. The terrain at sixty-eight hundred feet, where we stay, is mostly cloud forest, or somewhat higher, a stunted elfin forest of mosses and epiphytes. Of the birds we will see, four-fifths don't exist anywhere else.

What holds for birds holds equally for tribal life. A third of the population, and lord knows how many languages, are crammed, however precariously, into the several-thousand-foot clefts of a narrow plateau. Highly fertile volcanic soil has enabled the people to feed themselves until recently. And there still remains more than enough patchwork forest to satisfy the demands of the blue bird of paradise and Salvador's teal, the two species endangered by a restricted range.

Birds are normally early risers. It is easy to understand the reluctance of forest-edge birds to expose themselves to the insufferable brightness of a sun that, even by eight o'clock, has you frantically reaching for hat, sun cream, and Chapstick. They are, though, well adapted to the mist and rain that thunders every afternoon in spectacular mountain-and-sky silver-black explosions, turning the mud into a skating rink. The gray overcast may also explain the preponderance of black and velvet-black plumages. Yet feathers that appear black at a distance are often iridescent, the jewel-flashing turquoises and violets of birds of paradise.

In the Central Highlands, altitude determines what you find. Different plants grow at different elevations, and every few hundred feet up or down brings into life a new bird community. The higher you go, the more the flora narrows. But as certain plants drop out, others take over. Rhododendrons, for example, begin to appear only around eighty-five hundred feet. But because of the tropical climate there are more species in New

Guinea than even in Nepal—twenty-three in all. Most of them are epiphytic, an indication of how forbidding conditions are at this height. As to what alpine plants may still await higher up on more remote peaks, one can only guess. But there are real hazards to be overcome before any thoroughgoing botanical expedition can be mounted.

Not the least are those presented by people. Cannibalism was made a crime in 1949, saving in the nick of time at least one major tribe of brain eaters. But in higher and more remote valleys, eating someone can remain an indispensable ritual. The taxonomist Josef Halda tells of coming down from collecting seeds on a mountain and being presented with the bones of several of his bearers. While I was there, the authorities released from jail a man from an upper valley whom they had arrested for eating his wife. The man was impenitent. A time of year, he explained, had come around when he was required to eat someone. With no one else available, what could he do but eat his wife? With such beliefs, any passing stranger becomes fair game.

The Tari district is dominated by the Huhli wigmen, so called because of the elaborate daily rituals certain male societies undergo to fluff out their hair in fantastic feather-bright opulence. While a minority still go around naked except for a penis shaft and various feather-and-shell collars and ornaments, most are clothed, at the insistence of Seventh-day Adventists. I suspect it is not Christ, but the power of Western man they covet. Embracing Christianity gave them a way of stepping out of the Stone Age and into that of the airplane which so changed their lives. There was one old man who told me how he actually remembered the first one arriving, the beelike buzz with which it circled overhead. The Huhli still remain warriors, living in palisaded stockades featuring very long, barely one-man-wide entranceways, and when any dispute arises there they all are, redoubtable fellows armed to the teeth. Should you fail to pay an indemnity after running over a child, say, who has strayed into your path, you will be pursued even as far as Sydney, Australia, and killed. They are not folk to be trifled with.

While the men grow out their hair and parade around in extraordinary collections of feathers, the women's lot is not at all enviable. Seeing a number of pigs ranged outside a compound door—a payment clearly for some infraction—I asked what has happened. The man, I learned, had divorced one of his wives and the pigs were evidence she had returned all he had paid for her in bride-price.

The incident may help explain the great number of suicides among women in the Central Highlands. The women are mere slaves. Lacking any security, any way of feeling valued, suicide can seem to them the only possible solution. When a group of white people in their ghostly pallor pass before them—the "breath of the dead" as they, not unrightly, first named us—it is perhaps inevitable that wallets, guns, and magic prisms should fan resentment among tribespeople whose wealth is still largely measured in shells, feathers, and pigs. We caught some of this flak one early morning when our little bus rolled onto a much visited display site of Papua New Guinea's national bird, the raggiana bird of paradise. We stood around in a thick mist, surprised to be eyeing only one male instead of the three we had expected, when a man, clearly upset at being taken for granted, rushed up.

"How dare you," he sputtered out, "it is my land." Even more to the point, the male whose brief display we had come to savor (brief because the flashing of scarlet tail pennants, the back-and-forth throbbing of the strange velourlike flank feathers, requires much exertion as he dances from perch to perch) was his bird in that it displayed on his giant tree. And he showed us the feathers of its two competitors, recently cropped because they were needed for a sing-sing.

Did it do any good to point out that the display of a single male was a far cry from what three rivals would have produced? That was the glory of a spectacle we had caught by accident when a bunch of seemingly decaying yellow leaves in the unified green of the forest canopy a mile below turned out to be three male magnificent birds of paradise. Ranged one under the other, they were displaying before the critical eye of a female directly above. It was a real enactment for themselves, in the midst of nothing but hundreds of miles of rain forest; it felt, as we watched, as if the volleys of unearthly blue we witnessed were an avian rainbow, "magnificent" in the clear dawn.

It is worth noting that the *paradisiae* survived the millinery trade mainly because discerning collectors wanted only the best. The riffraff got off scot-free, and it's from the riffraff that stocks recovered once the ban on the feather trade began to be enforced.

The role that lions play in the African veldt in weeding out and thus strengthening the wildebeest, humans play in New Guinea. Some birds get cropped. Others are preserved for the qualities warriors value. They see them as gods, spirits a warrior can make himself into. We understood this intensely symbiotic give-and-take in the course of a sing-sing put on for us by some fifty tribesmen.

For about five hours I sat a few feet away from a couple of warriors who were using their own dyes and the feathers they had collected or traded to make themselves up. It was the care that went into getting each detail of a complex mask right that impressed, rather than the final enactment—a thundering line of shouting, leaping, flank-and-shoulder displaying warriors—which seemed, in its brevity, anticlimactic.

On our last morning, on the way to the Tari airstrip, our bus made a surprise stop in front of a tribal household. An old man, naked except for a penis shaft, escorted us down a series of muddy paths to where two other old men in similar traditional dress were awaiting us. (One of them turned out to be the local magistrate.) The household, we learned, boasted a display court of a Lawes parotia, or six-wired bird of paradise, a small chunky black bird less often seen than heard emitting crowlike caws as it clambered about in the canopy. The court, concealed in the midst of a patch of mountain oak, consisted of two strips of meticulously cleared earth separated from one another by a small tree. (Not far away lay a second court, disused now, that must have belonged to a competitor.)

While we sat on a couple of logs, a drum started in. Soon it was shaping a song the three men repeated over and over:

> *Parotia, you are very beautiful*
> *And we men are very beautiful*
> *Come join us at our sing-sing.*

After a few minutes, the parotia appeared. It flew in on silent wings and then dropped to its court. By lowering its head, the parotia raised six invisible head-wires attached to a blue spot on its nape. Then, after it had come closer and repeated the display, it vanished. Behind the parotia's appearance, there was no bribery other than the men's drumming and their offer of a song. Yet between the men and the bird there was a real exchange. It is not everywhere that the mere word, *beautiful,* casts such a web.

On Learning to Travel in a
Rock Garden
2000

The limestone outcropping next to my studio is quite small, barely six feet tall and measuring perhaps thirty feet from one end to the other. When I first came upon it, it was a mess of poison ivy, deeply embedded lily-of-the-valley, and wild ginger, flanked by two moribund ash trees; an unlikely site on which to try to establish a garden. Over the years I had tended a few plants here and there, but I would never have called myself a gardener, much less a rock gardener, a subject about which I knew nothing. But after forty years of writing, I welcomed anything that would unchain me from my desk. The prospect of an earth box of manageable size, rising up no more than a step from the door, proved irresistible.

In a prescient essay written in 1908, Victor Segalen remarked that, when worldwide travel becomes commonplace, there will always remain remote peaks where, among the mountain goats and the last unnamed flowers, the true explorers will be. At my age, I did not see myself clambering about on an uncataloged New Guinean mountainside. But on my outcropping I realized I could invite visitors from the far corners of the alpine plant world and found a settlement of specimens to assuage my wanderlust.

Once I had cut down the north ash tree and had cleared the soil as best I could, I should next have put in a porous, well-drained scree bed composed of four parts gravel to two parts earth and humus. But for the previous twenty years I had lived in France and England, and before that on the West Coast—

places where the mercury never descends much below freezing—
and I did not realize how drastically the sudden thaws and re-
freezings of a northwestern Connecticut winter could heave little
plants about, or what they might require in the way of siting,
light, protection, and drainage. And I was, I suppose, impatient.
All that concerned me was populating the clay of the little alp I
had unearthed with some appropriate plants.

A knowledgeable friend put me on to the Siskiyou catalog
from Oregon. Guided by their descriptions and zone indications,
I sent away for an instant garden of mountain flora. I joined
the local chapter of the Rock Garden Society and bore away as
many trays as I could from its monthly seedling sales. Any seedling
with a name new to me seemed worth trying; if it had been
grown locally, it might well be winter-hardy. What space remained, I filled with miniature garden perennials: dianthus, sea
thrift, phlox, cinquefoil, primulas, that kind of thing.

Since I had no idea how big the seedlings might grow, or
what conditions they required, there was much shifting about
before I got the right plants in the right sites. Not everything
tolerated my machinations. But a surprising number did, perhaps because their root systems were still so undeveloped I could
trowel beneath them. It was the collage aspect of rock gardening
I came to love the most, the constant adjustments, replacements,
and additions of an ongoing composition. Each time I moved a
plant I learned something about the kind of environment, the
kind of look I was, willy-nilly, creating.

I could get away with piecemeal dabbling because, unlike the
perennial border designer, I was not strewing around great swathes
of color and texture to create massed effects. I was merely trying
to situate single plants.

At least, I was starting out with single plants and, if they were
happy and sowed themselves about, so much the better. Unlike
the seasonal traveler, I could study the denizens of this artificial

landscape over time and learn what kinds of sites they wanted to inhabit. The tinier the plant, the more of a challenge the siting became; the more grave, too, the threat posed by a weed. But soon enough, I welcomed weeds and the excuse they gave to get down on my knees and actually make a new visual acquaintance, or pull out a label and learn what it was I had planted.

It helped that my outcropping was densely creviced, with a deep trough eroding the middle and several pronounced fissures made by the roots of the two ash trees. The shape of the rock dictated what would go where. The rock's height, and the shade cast by the remaining ash tree, suggested a narrow peat-and-humus-based woodland garden around the western and northern sides. To the east and south, where the rock gradually descended toward the lawn, I set up an alpine meadow of brawling taprooted thugs: poppies, phlox, pulsatilla, daisies, penstemons. When the dust cleared, I chose winners—anything beginning with the letter *p*.

Winter thaws brought a certain number of upended plants that kept having to be thrust back into their uncooperative soil, but by and large the plants were small enough that an inch or two of snow cover provided shelter enough from the worst winds. And when they began to come back from dormancy, we had none of the usual lethal frosts.

In a sense I may have been too lucky, for by the end of the second summer I had too many plants and was obliged to expand southeast into the lawn. I covered the grass with newspapers, laid on a foot and a half of soil and a few small boulders, and created an open garden in what I imagined to be the manner of the American Southwest. But of the plants that I either bought or transplanted into this raised bed, fewer than half survived the snowless winter of 1995. As a gardener presiding over a group of travelers, I had to be more systematic and deliberate in identifying the mountain plants and the kind of garden I wanted, and in redoing the soil to give them a drainage that would let them survive.

In starting a garden, my primary concern had been to find plants that would quickly fill it and look suitably alpine. Plants like creeping phlox, which cascade in tumbling waterfalls, helped fill in gaps while providing cover for spring bulbs to push through. The art, as I saw it, was to set one aggressive mat against the next and enjoy the resulting battlefield's riot of color.

But then I realized it was not the meadowland victors that enthralled me as much as the spectacle provided by their evolutionary victims, the tiny, compact-bodied cushion plants who had retreated to the more inaccessible screes and crevices of the topmost mountain ledges.

Up there, buffeted in near-permanent wind, with a window of six to eight weeks in which to grow, flower, and set seed, small size could be an advantage. The smaller a plant, the faster it could meet its survival needs. And the plant competed with its few neighbors through color, size, the whole complex spectacle of the flowers it offered pollinators. To a bee, big flowers or a mass of tiny flowers are the same. But there is the art of illusion, the frilly petals that make a flower look twice as large as it is.

Living on a tight budget, alpines cannot afford to shed their leaves and go dormant as most perennials do. For some, flowering was the final aria into which a beauty put all its remaining energy and died. A number of other scree dwellers either disappeared into the earth to await the next year's snow melt or developed a sweater of sorts in the form of an insulating cushion of hairs. The hairs enabled the plant to retain moisture in dry summers while providing a coat with which to ward off wintry blasts; the more exposed the habitat, the more ruffled or woolly the coat.

The startling beauty of alpine flowers, the gray or silvery foliage and compact perfection of the plants, the way they tumble from ledges and dance over rock, all that beguiled me. As Reginald Farrer writes, "There is something about these tiny plants that makes us their slaves." Unlike most gardeners, who need plants large enough to stop you in your tracks, I did not see smallness as an obstacle. Small plants do not consume a lot of garden. The taller the mound you give them, the more potential ledges you have with which to establish different viewing areas and separate one species from another. The resulting shadows, the different angles cast by the sun striking one or another rock or ledge, in turn create their own microclimates.

I may not be able to grow a whole mountaintop world in a grain of sand. But using microclimates I can accommodate in several thousand such grains a substantial bit of it: April-to-June-flowering gems from the Rockies, Pyrenees, Alps, Turkey, and the Caucasus; matted midseason bloomers from arctic tundra, the Falklands, and Patagonia; fall gentians from China; and a host of others that emerge in New Mexico, the Himalayas, and South Africa after monsoons to extend a flowering season. They retain a scent of faraway habitats I must respect if I am to keep them around. Perhaps Maurice Maeterlinck was right; with an alpine garden in my backyard there is no compelling need to travel.

At the end of the second winter, the remaining ash tree had to be cut down. My caretaker and I dug out the surrounding clay to a depth of four feet and installed a steeply inclined sand bed and a scree composed of equal parts pebbles and earth. The virtue of sand, other than offering a lovely softness to kneel and plant in, is that it helps retain water. But soil that never dries out can rot any plant not set high enough for the wet to drain away.

With a scree, I can grow most alpine plants, anything that does not require a lime-free, acid-based soil. And I can insert pebbles into the crevice pockets if a leaner habitat is called for. In blazing afternoon sun, the scree reminds me of the dried torrent bed below Mount Ida in Crete where I once ruined a friend's motor scooter taking a hitchhiker to a country wedding.

The depth of soil—four feet—may have been unnecessary, but alpine plants are delicately tendriled, and a substantial bed gives their roots room to forage, while the boulders strewn torrentlike over the surface provide crevices that keep them cool in summer and sheltered from winter winds.

After putting in the two new beds, I dug out the remaining clay and constructed a neighboring pair of little mountains that mirrored the outcropping. Now plants could pop out from different angles, one astonishment succeeding another. Those too small to hold their own in the open garden went onto a bench of troughs outside the studio. An artificial solution, but there at least they were protected in porous tufa and placed high enough to be seen.

By now, I realized I had become a miniaturist. Anything over six inches tall was dispatched to the perennial border, but my penchant for miniature plants left a design problem. If I stacked boulders in receding tiers, by the time the crevices were high enough, the plants were too far away to be seen. Troughs were a solution, but I only had so many, and besides, I wanted my plants in the garden, not in separate containers.

The solution was to construct, in the mixed shade of my studio, a berm that continued the outcropping in the form of a ledge garden. In circumference, the berm was not very much bigger than what my arms could reach, kneeling on the grass outside. Yet the ledges of thin rock descending in parallel walls provided a well-drained runoff that kept water from collecting around the crown, while protecting the plant in a crevice pocket. If need be, I could tilt the ledge wall at an angle to provide a roof against the wet. In these shaded conditions, the ledges made glittering backdrops that brought warmth while allowing all but the tiniest plants to be lit up and thus seen.

A fellow gardener once remarked that, in her acquaintance, there are as many varieties of rock gardens as there are gardeners, and each expresses the gardener exactly. For me, a ledge garden offers something like the possibilities of a picture book, brilliant juxtapositions that you move away from or come back to, individual pockets broken now and then by the two-page spread of a tiny larch or the oddness of a group of cylindrical cacti. The multitude of partitions lets me cram in as much as I can of miniature beauty and surprise and grotesque astonishment and somehow or other get away with it.

Nonetheless that "somehow or other" bothers me. For a couple of years I kept lists of the plants I had killed, grateful that I was a gardener and not a surgeon. It may be too much to expect a plant to look as good in my garden as it does on a faraway mountainside. In thinner air the blue of a gentian has an unearthly quality I can't possibly reproduce. As for the environment, there is only so much I can control. Some plants are happy and return every year; others, despite everything, give up the ghost.

But just as a garden goes through stages, so does the gardener. It is an art you can learn, but only when you have evolved, traveled, and seen enough to be ready for a next step. In the process you are always experimenting, inserting A into B's site while banishing C—an emperor constantly fussing with tiny beleaguered citizens. The longer you persist, the more you realize it's not you, but plants that generate their own proximities. In the long run, the garden is less yours than theirs, and your task is to keep it free of invasive competition, open to auspicious influences. You may not be able to grow everything from all over the mountain world you want to, but you can certainly try. And killing plants has to be part of the learning process.

Besides learning about plants themselves, what conditions they can and cannot abide, there is inevitably an aesthetic side. If alpine gardening is an art, it is because one aims at perfection.

When every weed is a menace and you are dealing with very small plants, nothing less will do. You can define a look, a mountain abundance, which you are trying, plant by plant, to reproduce. But beauty requires choices, and every time I get down on my knees in the garden I make them. In choosing, I inevitably learn something about design itself, all that goes into the composition I undertake.

At the same time, gardening changes something in me as well. In our society, we tend to drive or run past tiny plants, which, admittedly, are hard to see. But once I'm on my knees, the big picture vanishes and I enter a world different from the one I know standing up. As its plants enlarge, so do I. If I wish, I can haul out a hand lens and refine still further the same rabbit's-eye perspective, Or I can try to record a flowering moment with a picture, one way at least of certifying that I actually grew a fabled specimen.

The shift in perspective brings one in time as well. Down on my knees, *I* become rooted. There is only so far I can travel. Like it or not, I start seeing things from a plant's own perspective. It is not time itself that matters, but the soothing warmth of the dirt in my hands, the play of the light on my back and shoulders, as I prop myself with one hand and pluck with the other. People talk about *working* in their gardens. For me, it is more like *playing*. I am out there enjoying the very different lights of a spring or midsummer or Indian summer day. And I invent tasks, such as collecting seeds, so I can stay out longer and watch the blues of penstemons emerge in twilight shadows. The wind, the swirling gnats, the light, the garden's restricted, concentrated space, make me feel all the more intensely present and alive. That's what every tiny alpine plant is, and what it gives me.

Acknowledgments

Earlier versions of the introduction and "On Learning to Travel in a Rock Garden" appeared in *Southwest Review* and *Rock Garden Quarterly,* respectively. Much of "Samarkand, Bukhara, Khiva" appeared as *Fabled Cities of Central Asia* (Abbeville, 1990). Early versions of the Greek, Russian, Zambian, Madagascan, Nepalese, and Burgandian essays appeared in *And Other Voyages* (Mho and Mho Works, 1986).

About the Author

Robin Magowan is the author of *America, America; Memoirs of a Minotaur; Lilac Cigarette in a Wish Cathedral; Tour de France;* and *Fabled Cities of Central Asia: Samarkand, Bukhara, Khiva.* He is also the translator of Henri Michaux's *Ecuador.* He lives in Salisbury, Connecticut.